EMBODY

Other Abingdon Press Books by Karoline M. Lewis

SHE: Five Keys to Unlock the Power of Women in Ministry

SHE Participant Book: Five Keys to Unlock the Power of Women in Ministry

KAROLINE M. LEWIS

EMBODY

FIVE KEYS TO
LEADING WITH INTEGRITY

Abingdon Press™

Nashville

EMBODY:
FIVE KEYS TO LEADING WITH INTEGRITY

Copyright © 2020 by Abingdon Press

ISBN: 978-1-5018-9942-3

Library of Congress Control Number: 2020935151

Scripture quotations unless noted otherwise are from the Common English Bible. Copyright © 2011 by the Common English Bible. All rights reserved. Used by permission. www.CommonEnglishBible.com.

Scripture quotations noted NRSV are taken from the New Revised Standard Version Bible, copyright © 1989 National Council of the Churches of Christ in the United States of America. Used by permission. All rights reserved worldwide. http://nrsvbibles.org/.

From pages 2–3, "Blessing the Body" © Jan Richardson from *The Painted Prayerbook* (paintedprayerbook. com). Used by permission.

From page 54, William Stafford, "The Way It Is" from *Ask Me: 100 Essential Poems*. Copyright © 1977, 2014 by William Stafford and the Estate of William Stafford. Used with the permission of The Permissions Company, LLC on behalf of Kim Stafford and Graywolf Press, Minneapolis, Minnesota, graywolfpress.org..

From pages 55–56, "For a Leader" from TO BLESS THE SPACE BETWEEN US: A BOOK OF BLESSINGS by John O'Donohue, copyright © 2008 by John O'Donohue. Used by permission of Doubleday, an imprint of the Knopf Doubleday Publishing Group, a division of Penguin Random House LLC. All rights reserved.

From Page 84, poem by Annie Langseth, copyright © 2020 by Annie Langseth. Used with permission.

From pages 105–06, "For One Who Holds Power" from TO BLESS THE SPACE BETWEEN US: A BOOK OF BLESSINGS by John O'Donohue, copyright © 2008 by John O'Donohue. Used by permission of Doubleday, an imprint of the Knopf Doubleday Publishing Group, a division of Penguin Random House LLC. All rights reserved.

From page 134, Amy Schmidt, "Abundance," Poets Respond, January 20, 2019, https://www.rattle.com /respond/, accessed February 15, 202.

From pages 136–37, "The Magdalene's Blessing" © Jan Richardson from *Circle of Grace: A Book of Blessings for the Seasons*. Orlando, FL: Wanton Gospeller Press. Used by permission. janrichardson.com.

From pages 168–69, "Blessed Are You Who Bear the Light" © Jan Richardson from *Circle of Grace: A Book of Blessings for the Seasons*. Orlando, FL: Wanton Gospeller Press. Used by permission. janrichardson.com.

20 21 22 23 24 25 26 27 28 29 -- 10 9 8 7 6 5 4 3 2 1

MANUFACTURED IN THE UNITED STATES OF AMERICA

CONTENTS

PREFACE

Riches I Hold In Light Esteem

Riches I hold in light esteem
And Love I laugh to scorn
And lust of Fame was but a dream
That vanished with the morn—

And if I pray, the only prayer
That moves my lips for me
Is—'Leave the heart that now I bear
And give me liberty.'

Yes, as my swift days near their goal
'Tis all that I implore—
Through life and death a chainless soul
With courage to endure![1]

    —Emily Brontë

---

1. Emily Brontë, "Riches I Hold in Light Esteem," in *Brontë Sisters: Selected Poems*, ed. Stevie Davies (New York: Routledge, 2002).

PREFACE

Embody recognizes and names an unspoken truth of pastors and other leaders in the church: how frequently we find ourselves trapped in church systems and institutions where our actions and our decisions often seem to have little to do with the scriptures to which we are supposed to give authority or with the theology we profess. The church is indeed an institution, thereby requiring systems in place to keep it running, or even to keep it alive. Yet increasingly, the church finds itself adopting or adapting to systems devoid of theology or uninterested in faith altogether. Swept up into leadership norms that resemble business models more than the gospel mission, the church and its leaders have become hardly recognizable as faith-oriented or gospel-centered. In our efforts to be relevant, to acclimate ourselves to the changing times, to survive in contemporary society, we grasp at those proverbial straws, at whatever innovative or exciting program might secure success.

Terms like *innovation, best practices, marketing, enterprise, profits,* and *the bottom line* have replaced *creation, discipleship, apostolicity, church, evangelism,* and *salvation.* Innovation in particular has become the solution to declining church membership, dwindling seminary enrollment, and the church's diminishing relevance. Yet, the following critique is worth considering when it comes to leadership and the church: "Innovation and disruption are ideas that originated in the arena of business but which have since been applied to arenas whose values and goals are remote from the values and goals of business."[2] Abandoned is our characteristic theological vocabulary. We have given in to these models and frameworks, desperate for that which might increase the numbers and thereby save the church. That next shiny new thing just might be the answer—except that we have forgotten the question.

At this critical juncture of church in the post-Christendom era, there is a crisis. It is a crisis, however, not of the death of the church but a crisis of leadership. The church has always been a voice sounding from the margins, and yet most leadership efforts today are attempts to bring the church to the center. Once the church is indistinguishable from the rest of society, it has ceased to be the church.

This crisis of leadership can be defined succinctly: there is a disconnect between theology and leadership, between core theological commitments and the practices of ministry. Leaders in the church seem unable to integrate fully their beliefs with their behavior, their faith with the daily functions of ministry. We know we need to be and do what we believe. We know we need to embody our Christian beliefs in every decision, in every act of ministry leadership. But somewhere along the line, we became convinced of mainstream solutions for church membership, church growth, or church programming that can have little do with the Bible and theology. How we lead, both within congregations and in the public square, demonstrates whether or not the Bible matters for the church's mission in the world. How can leadership in the church live out a direct line between what we believe theologically and what we do for the sake of God's church?

If you are reading this book, then perhaps you share this disillusionment and disintegration. Maybe you are aware of this disconnect in your own leadership, but you have not been able to name it, or, if you have,

2. Jill Lepore, "The Disruption Machine," *The New Yorker*, June 16, 2014, https://www.newyorker.com/magazine/2014/06/23/the-disruption-machine.

then you are not sure what to do about it. This disjuncture is difficult to articulate because the absence of integrity, that is, the inability to embody one's theological commitments in actions of leadership, hovers very closely to hypocrisy. We remember what Jesus said about hypocrisy. We are accomplished in pointing it out in others. But it is another issue altogether to have to admit it in ourselves. Now is a precarious occasion for leadership in the church because we have convinced ourselves that this lack of integration is not hypocrisy. In fact, however, it is hypocrisy—albeit subtle enough to pretend it is not there. And when leadership in the church buys into characteristics of and models for leadership outside of the church it comes dangerously close to committing idolatry.

There are many metaphors we can use for leadership in the church, and yet those from the business world—CEO, coach, mentor—would be completely foreign to Jesus. A number of different metaphors have been applied to Jesus's ministry, and therefore, to Jesus's leadership—king, Lord, shepherd, Messiah, and teacher. According to the Gospel of John, when it comes to the metaphor Jesus himself uses to describe his ministry and the leadership of his movement, Jesus chooses an image that designates the primary work of the Holy Spirit—the *paraclete*.

In John 14:6, Jesus says, "I will ask the Father, and he will send another Companion, who will be with you forever." The word *companion* translates the Greek word *paraclete*, a compound noun that conjoins *para*, which means "alongside of" and *klētos*, which means "to call." Unique to John's Gospel, Jesus portrays his own leadership as walking alongside those he leads. The *paraclete* is the Holy Spirit whom Jesus will send to be with the disciples in his absence but also who Jesus himself has been for his disciples throughout his ministry. How can the idea of *paraclete* function as the primary metaphor for leadership in the church? How might Jesus as *paraclete* be our biblical mandate for leadership? Embodying *paraclete* leadership, a metaphor that Jesus himself uses, can be the first step toward leading with integrity. As such, the theological foundation for integration is the incarnation, the Word becoming flesh. When we take the incarnation seriously, then integrity is more likely because integrity is the embodied expression of the incarnation. When we consider the *paraclete* as an image for leadership as embodied by Jesus, the Word incarnate, in the Fourth Gospel, five key principles emerge: accompaniment, attentiveness, authenticity, abundance, and advocacy. These key principles are not only embodied by Jesus but also by five women characters in the Gospel of John with whom Jesus interacts. The mother of Jesus, the Samaritan woman at the well, Martha, Mary, and Mary Magdalene help us see what embodiment and integrity look like as a believer.

The topic of leadership has always intrigued me, often because I have found it difficult to define. Maybe you picked up this book because someone has told you that you would make a great leader and you wonder just exactly what that means, especially a leader in the church. Maybe you were placed in a leadership role, and you have found yourself asking: Now what? Maybe you have backed into leadership roles and now need a dialogue partner to figure out who you are as a leader and who God needs you to be as a leader. Or maybe you have known great leaders and really poor leaders and have asked yourself: Just what determines a good leader from a bad leader?

My hope for this book is that it can be a conversation partner for you as you lean into your own understanding of leadership, especially as you imagine and construct your theology of leadership. *Embody* certainly does not exhaust the possibilities of what leadership might look like in the church. But perhaps it can call attention to the importance of intentional reflection about leadership, especially in the church, and the necessity of biblical and theological reflection so as to lead with integrity. At stake in our leadership is the ability of the church to embody God's love in and for the world.

I am grateful once again for Abingdon Press and its invitation to work on this project. I am especially grateful for my editor, Connie Stella, and her unwavering belief in what I have to say. To the hosts of my writing retreat, Gwen Fulsang and Mike Alexander, thank you. They made writing in the midst of teaching and seminary demands possible, making sure I was well fed and keeping me accountable to my promised daily word count. The gift of knowing a leader with theological integrity, who embodies all five of the Spirit's companionship—accompaniment, attentiveness, authenticity, abundance, and advocacy—is a rare gift indeed. That leader for me was my doctoral advisor, Dr. Gail R. O'Day—John scholar, author, preacher, teacher, administrator, feminist, and friend. Because of her companionship, I hold myself to the high standard of leadership that God, and the church, calls forth. Gail, this book is for and because of you.

Karoline M. Lewis
Pentecost 2019

INTRODUCTION

Blessing the Body

This blessing takes
    one look at you
    and all it can say is
    holy.
Holy hands.
    Holy face.
    Holy feet.
    Holy everything
    in between.
Holy even in pain.
    Holy even when weary.
    In brokenness, holy.
    In shame, holy still.
Holy in delight.
    Holy in distress.
    Holy when being born.
    Holy when we lay it down
    at the hour of our death.
So, friend,
    open your eyes
    (holy eyes).
    For one moment
    see what this blessing sees,
    this blessing that knows
    how you have been formed
    and knit together
    in wonder and
    in love.

Welcome this blessing
    that folds its hands
    in prayer
    when it meets you;
    receive this blessing
    that wants to kneel
    in reverence
    before you:
    you who are
    temple,
    sanctuary,
    home for God
    in this world.[1]

    —Jan Richardson

---

1. "Blessing the Body" © Jan Richardson from *The Painted Prayerbook* (paintedprayer book.com). Used by permission.

INTRODUCTION

*The vocation of pastor(s) has been replaced by the strategies
of religious entrepreneurs with business plans.*

—Eugene H. Peterson

A quick Google search reveals that there is no shortage of books out there on leadership. The myriad of titles promises success in leadership, offering steps toward effective leadership and techniques to reach your potential as a leader. Leadership is the topic of the day, so it is no surprise that it has found its way into the church. A pastor is indeed a leader, one who shapes the ethos of a congregation through preaching and teaching but also through administration and decision making. People look to their pastor for guidance and counsel, for direction and vision.

There is nothing inherently wrong with these various resources. In a day and age when the church tries to maintain its relevance in an increasingly secular world, it is no wonder the church's leaders turn to means by which the rest of society's leadership seems to have gained a footing. Companies and businesses appear to have a better sense of how to navigate effectual leadership in the midst of changing times. Employing their failsafe strategies can only help the church and not hurt it, right?

Wrong. Since the church's earliest days as a community struggling to survive in the midst of a dominant imperial cult, it has always been the church's challenge to determine how it can adjust, both to survive and thrive. We witness in the New Testament writings the negotiation between the pressures of the controlling society and holding on to the specificities of the Christian life. A rough chronological survey of New Testament books shows that the later writings must concern themselves with order and structure particularly once communities begin to realize that they may be around longer than they had originally imagined. As a result, different roles for leaders in the community were implemented, such as presbyters and bishops. For example, in 1 Peter we read: "Therefore, I have a request for the elders among you. (I ask this as a fellow elder and a witness of Christ's sufferings, and as one who shares in the glory that is about to be revealed.) I urge the elders…" (5:1); in James, we read: "If any of you are sick, they should call for the elders of the church, and the elders should pray over them, anointing them with oil in the name of the Lord" (5:14); and in 1 Timothy: "This saying is reliable: if anyone has a goal to be a supervisor in the church, they want a good thing" (3:1).

In these verses, we see a transition to hierarchical order taking place as the concerns of fledgling congregations move from theological and Christological issues to doctrinal and organizational issues. The church has always had to fight for its unique identity. It has always had to figure out how to distinguish itself amid the chatter of its surroundings, especially those surroundings that have considerably more power and leverage than any ecclesial voice ever will. As the church moved forward into the centuries, it was pressed to define itself over and against the heresies of the day. As such, the church's hand has frequently been forced, reacting to circumstances rather than proactively acting to distinguish its core beliefs. How will the church describe itself, and by what qualities will it characterize its structures? How will the church define its identity? How will the church be distinctively faith-based and faith-oriented without being exclusive or prideful? And at what point in these navigations has the cost been too much, a kind of watered-down credo where the church seems to have lost sight of its heart?

Distinctiveness is essential for all institutions, especially for the sake of survival. The church is not exempt from the demand of differentiation. At the same time, however, the church has a rather unfortunate history of adopting and adapting, sometimes to its detriment. Paul's injunction in 1 Corinthians is an example of how the church embraced societal norms: "...the women should be quiet during the meeting. They are not allowed to talk. Instead, they need to get under control, just as the Law says. If they want to learn something, they should ask their husbands at home. It is disgraceful for a woman to talk during the meeting. Did the word of God originate with you? Has it come only to you?" (14:34-36). Regardless of scholarly interpretations arguing that these verses were not in the original letter, explained as a later interpolation, their damage has outweighed justification of their insertion. The adaptation and adoption have had a historically negative effect, particularly when it comes to the leadership and ordination of women in the church.

In both Ephesians and Colossians, we see the author(s) suggesting Greco-Roman household codes for structuring a Christian household (Eph 5:21-33; Col 3:18-25). Once again, although biblical scholars argue that these passages were the church's solution to assimilation, these texts are used to validate the subordination of women. In other words, the church has a history of assimilating ideas, forms, terminology, modalities, methods, structures, and so on that at first blush seem to be benign solutions for subsistence. But such adaptions are never without consequences. There has always been the threat of the church losing its distinctiveness at best and, at worst, losing its voice entirely.

A point of clarification here is necessary. This is not an argument to get the church back to what it used to be before the world messed it up, before the encroachment of the Roman Empire, or before its inevitable institutionalization. There is no pristine church or idyllic ecclesial leadership to which we can harken back and, therefore, use to solve the problem of how the church exists and persists in a world mostly uninterested in its values. The church has always had to differentiate itself theologically, institutionally, and organizationally. Those who are loyal to and leading in the church are charged with tending where and how this demand works itself out. *Embody* tells the truth about how the church responds to this necessity by taking on the wardrobe of the world, which then makes it indistinguishable as a church apart from society's values.

And so, the church dons doctrinal rigidity.

It wears claims about its scripture, which scripture has never made about itself.

It puts on the attire of the culture, sometimes to blend in, as it had to do in the past, and sometimes in an effort to garner the kind of pertinence for which it has always wished.

The intent of *Embody* is not to retrieve some utopian ecclesial leadership model, a pre-corruption time of Jesus, or an ideal never grounded in reality. Rather, *Embody* suggests that the church's leadership is called to model the dialectic that is the constant struggle between core commitments and survival. The church is called to be an example of how Christian communities must always plot a course between what God needs it to be and what the church presumes the world wants it to be. Leadership in the church can never be a quick fix, or any fix at all. The church always exists in the tension between what God calls it to be and what it supposes it has to be.

The church's vocation is to model a way of leadership in the world that has an inherently different purpose, and that purpose is not a secular understanding of success. Success for the church is embodying a way of being in the world that gives witness to the abiding presence of God. For the church, leadership is not a noun but a verb, not a set of characteristics but an expression of who God is and how God works in the world, not a taxonomy of traits but a living out of the Kingdom of God in our midst. Leadership in the church can never be static but must always evaluate where and how its leadership structures are prone to idolatry.

Church institutions assume they are being theological in their leadership when they say things such as, "The Holy Spirit is calling Grace Lutheran Church to..." But this is an extraordinarily presumptive claim. Furthermore, such claims are one-sided. They lack demonstrated activity of connecting theological thought to the church's mission or vision. These kinds of claims do indeed reveal our idea of who God is and, in this case, God's work can be codified, assessed, and even predicted.

A FEW MORE WORDS ABOUT LEADERSHIP

Integrity is choosing courage over comfort; it's choosing what's right over what's fun, fast, or easy; and it's practicing your values, not just professing them.

—Brené Brown

What word might church leaders use instead of *leadership,* given that the word *leader* has a rather iniquitous presence in the New Testament? The term typically translated as "leader" or "ruler" is predominantly cast in negative terms: perceived opponents of Jesus and the gospel (Matt 20:25; Luke 14:1; 23:13, 35; 24:20; John 3:1; 7:48; 12:42; Acts 4:26; 13:27; 14:5); associated with Satan or the devil (Matt 9:34; 12:24; Mark 3:22; Luke 11:15; John 12:31; 14:30; 16:11); and rulers of this age (1 Cor 2:6, 8; Eph 2:2). Only in Revelation is the term used in reference to Jesus: "And from Jesus Christ—the faithful witness, the firstborn from among the dead, and the ruler of the kings of the earth" (Rev 1:5). There are, of course, various terms and metaphors for designated leaders of God's people throughout scripture, and God's people have a complicated history of figuring out just what kind of leader they want. From Moses to the judges to the prophets to the kings, exactly what the Israelites desire in a leader has always been rather unclear. When it comes to the New Testament, Paul uses various metaphors to describe his oversight of the churches he has founded ("apostle" 1 Cor 1:1, Gal 1:1; "father" 1 Cor 4:15, Phlm 10; "nursing mother" 1 Thess 2:7). The New Testament's later writings reveal the early church's struggle to figure out a leadership structure in light of the realization that the church would be here for a while. It is in these correspondences that we see words such as *presbyter* and *bishop* (1 Pet 5:1; 1 Tim 3:2). In other words, when it comes to overseeing a community existing because of God's love, there is an observable fluidity in the church's attempts to identify a fitting kind of leadership. Perhaps this is how it should be. Once leadership becomes overly prescribed in the church, it loses its Spirit-driven identity. The challenge, therefore, is finding a way to talk about leadership in the church that maintains a certain mutability but also articulates some basic principles so the church does not get lost in variability.

To some extent, when the church claimed *leadership* as a word for supervising positions held in the church, it muddied the waters somewhat. Employing mainstream vocabulary can be helpful and is sometimes even necessary when the church tries to locate its place and voice in society. At the same time, it is easy to embrace indistinctiveness of vocabulary around leadership, thereby losing sight of how the church is unique in its expressions and manifestations of leadership.

As a result, the church's intentional reference to, and use of, the Bible and theology is essential for the church's understanding and description of leadership. A biblical or theological imagination for leadership is indeed what makes leadership in the church distinctive. The church is the only institution that can make these connections, that can give witness to leadership models founded on the language of scripture and grounded in the continuity of God. When the church lets go of this prophetic responsibility, its accountability to the Bible and to its theological commitments will, and should, fall under scrutiny. As Jill Lepore writes, "Transfixed by change, [disruptive innovation] is blind to continuity. It makes a very poor prophet."[2]

While we have touched on presentations of leadership in the Old Testament and in some New Testament writings, we have yet to address Jesus as leader. Of course, what kind of leader people want him to be and what kind of leader Jesus describes himself to be makes for an interesting comparison, both in the New Testament writings and in today's conversation. Expectations were high for Jesus's leadership, particularly in the Gospels, because who Jesus is as a leader is also caught up in Jesus's identity. Is Jesus Elijah, the one whose role it was to usher in the reign of the Messiah? Is Jesus the Anointed One? The anticipated King of the Jews? A new David? In other words, how Jesus leads is connected to, and interwoven with, his identity. When Jesus's leadership seems to conflict with his assumed identity, and when his perceived identity appears to be at odds with his behavior, then this conflict ends up being the crux of both a polemic and a resistance.

Over the course of the Gospel narratives, Jesus uses a number of metaphors, directly and indirectly, making self-referential descriptions of his role and mission. Jesus's role and mission constitute an array of images deeply rooted in his scriptures, the Hebrew Bible. As a result, there are certain images to which Jesus refers that we would expect, such as king and shepherd but not leader, and titles alone are not enough to capture who Jesus will be as a leader of this new movement within Judaism. Throughout the Gospels, few adjectives are used to describe Jesus, and they are frustratingly ambiguous. For example, no biblical scholar knows quite what to do with Jesus's claim to be the "good" shepherd in John 10. What exactly makes Jesus "good"?

---

2. Jill Lepore, "The Disruption Machine," *The New Yorker*, June 16, 2014, https://www.newyorker.com/magazine/2014/06/23/the-disruption-machine.

Jesus is described verbally. Jesus is not compassionate; rather, he had compassion. As we read in Matthew: "Now Jesus called his disciples and said, 'I feel sorry [compassionate] for the crowd because they have been with me for three days and have nothing to eat. I don't want to send them away hungry for they won't have enough strength to travel'" (15:32). Or, as we also read in Luke: "When he saw her, the Lord had compassion for her and said, 'Don't cry'" (7:13). What difference does this make for how the church does leadership? It means that summarizing one's leadership is not as simple as providing a list of adjectives. More often than not, we succumb to offering a catalog of our greatest traits to define our leadership style—relational, organized, hardworking, good preacher, good teacher—and nowhere in that set of skills is any articulation of the relationship between that trait and one's theological commitments.

Among the parade of metaphors for Jesus's leadership is a gem of a verse that gets the closest to Jesus's own articulation of what it means to be a leader: "I will ask the Father, and he will send another Companion, who will be with you forever" (John 14:16). As noted in the preface, the word translated "companion" is the Greek word *paraclete*, literally, the one called to be alongside or beside. Though penned by John, we at least have witness to Jesus's self-reflection of who he was and how he was among his followers. Knowing that he will no longer be with his disciples, Jesus realizes that they will need another leader—the *paraclete*.

It is no accident that this promise from Jesus takes place during what is known in the Fourth Gospel as the "Farewell Discourse." These five chapters, framed by Jesus washing his disciples' feet (chapter 13) and the "High Priestly Prayer" (chapter 17), are Jesus at his pastoral best. Jesus knows the chain of events that will follow when he says in John 10:14, "the good shepherd" lays down his life for the sheep. The disciples need to be comforted and then need to be prepared. Jesus's clearest reflection about his own ministry and thereby on his own leadership occurs in a moment of pastoral care.

That leadership in the church is born out of a perceived need for pastoral care is a critical component for how the church thinks about leadership and trains leaders. We see Paul's leadership at work in response to worries he has for his churches. His own sense of his role within the churches he founded is often dependent on concerns within, and concerns for, his congregations; Paul is able to practice leadership in nuanced ways in response to the issues at hand. Paul's theology is a work in progress; it is dependent on the intersection of a church's theological assumptions and how Paul assumes God might act in, and respond to, these potential theological crises.

Leadership as the expression or embodiment of pastoral care is also true of Jesus's description of the *paraclete*. After the first reference to the *paraclete*, Jesus then defines the role of the *paraclete* not with adjectives but with what the *paraclete* will actually do. The *paraclete* will teach the disciples everything and remind them of all that Jesus has said to them (John 14:26). The *paraclete* will testify on Jesus's behalf (15:26); the *paraclete* will prove the world wrong about sin, righteousness, and judgment (16:8-11); the *paraclete* will guide the disciples in all truth and declare the things that are to come (16:13); and, finally, the *paraclete* will glorify Jesus (16:14).

Jesus's articulation of the *paraclete's* activities is reflective of the root meaning of the term. Again, as a compound word, *para* means "alongside of" and *klētos* comes from the Greek verb *kaleō*, which means "to call." The *paraclete*, therefore, is the one called to be alongside us, to walk alongside us, to accompany us, to stand beside us, and to be our companion. As a result, the word *paraclete* can be, and has been, translated as *advocate*, *comforter*, *aider*, *intercessor*, *guider*, *teacher*, *supporter*, and *counselor*.

Instead of the church using the word *leader*, how might our perception of leadership, both within and from without, shift if we were to employ the word Jesus used to describe his ministry over those three years? What would happen if the church chose to utilize a term that Jesus himself called upon to identify his own leadership? What if the church committed to using *paraclete* instead of *leader*? How might that fundamentally alter how we talk about leadership and go about leading in the church?

Church leadership has tried to compete with expectations of leadership that society wants, accepts, and appreciates. Predominantly, this is a kind of leadership that is in control, organized, and strategic—and none of these adjectives even begin to define Jesus's ministry. In fact, when Jesus appears to be describing his ministry, he is the least in control. We might even say that integrity in leadership is born out of crisis, as leaders in the church know well from the coronavirus pandemic, for example. The Farewell Discourse is a swirl of human emotions, both for the disciples and for Jesus. Jesus knows that the hour has arrived; in John 13:1 we read: "Before the Festival of Passover, Jesus knew that his time [hour] had come to leave this world and go to the Father. Having loved his own who were in the world, he loved them fully." The entire Farewell Discourse is an anticipation of Jesus's departure and an assurance for the disciples that Jesus will not abandon them. Jesus washes the disciples' feet, even Judas's feet (who betrays him only verses later), and Peter's (whose denial Jesus predicts in the very same chapter). There is nothing in control, organized, or strategic about the Farewell Discourse, with the exception of Jesus being fully aware of his fate. How the disciples will respond, how Jesus will respond to their emotions, cannot be scripted. The final chapter (chapter 17) is a compendium of uncertainty. In this three-part prayer, Jesus prays for himself, for his disciples, and for believers yet to be. Prayer happens when you realize that you are *not* in control. There is no other thing to do, no other place to go, except to turn to God.

WHY INTEGRITY?

Jesus was not killed by atheism and anarchy. He was brought down by law
and order allied with religion—which is always a deadly mix. Beware those
who claim to know the will of God and are prepared to use force, if necessary,
to make others conform. Beware those who cannot tell
God's will from their own.

—Barbara Brown Taylor

Integrity in church leadership is essential. The hallmark of this integrity, an ecclesial integrity if you will, is being able to identify a biblical or theological imagination for leadership. If there is no clear theological or biblical foundation for one's professed leadership in the church, then there will be nothing distinctive in church leaders, especially when compared to every kind of other leader out there in the world. The church has always had as its call a sense of being set apart, but not for superiority, not to out-lead the competition, and not for an inimitability or "better than" existence. When the church views itself in these ways, then it truly is no different than the current business market, no different than the buzz of capitalism, no different than the commerce that determines best practices, no different than what tries, at every turn, to persuade with an eye toward perceived universal human desires.

The church has always been about distinctiveness, not exclusivity. About particularity, not partisanship. About relationship, not metrics. Integrity matters for the church's imagination for its leadership because it is lodged in the specificity of the incarnation, the Word that has been made flesh. As such, the incarnation acknowledges a theology of vulnerability and not of force, a theology of liability and not of power. The great reversal that God became human commits to instability, not to certainty. The truth we are seeking cannot be fixed propositions but will always be an experiential Truth. In the end, to prioritize the incarnation means that theology is not arguing over views of God but is a way of being in the world that points out how far the world is from the Kingdom of God. What is that observable difference of church leaders? *Embody* seeks to define and categorize that difference. Our language needs to be different. Our philosophy has to be different. How we speak about leading needs to be different.

The integration of theology and how we lead has to be visible in church leaders—a starting point that is grounded theologically and biblically, that has an imagination inspired by God's very presence in all that we say and do. A unique characteristic of church leaders, therefore, is an unquestionable visibility of active theology, a kind of "doing of theology" that is demonstrated in leaders' behaviors and decisions. It is leadership that is animated by the expectation of God's constancy and consistency. It is a dialectical and dialogical leadership, a leadership that manifests as an ongoing conversation with God.

Without a direct correlation between a leader's professed biblical or theological imagination and a leader's rhetoric and behavior is the possible accusation of hypocrisy. Without that observed correlation, trust is threatened, as that which motivates and encourages, which shapes and forms, which is consulted and incorporated is called into question. Without this ecclesial integrity, the source of one's motivations could very well be a source or a voice far less faithful than our God.

The church leader serves from this integrated space, which is a dynamic place revealing a synergy between the incarnated God and God incarnated in our witness. In other words, we do not apply theological characteristics to our leadership, but our leadership embodies particular characteristics of God. What are these characteristics? That is for the church leader to decide based on biblical and theological reflection. The critical issue is that you lead from that place of theological identity and integrity.

The premise of this book is simple: that leadership in the church should be distinctive from other models and forms of leadership. The difference can be summarized clearly in this way: that leaders in the church are intentional about how their core theological convictions shape and define how they lead. We might describe this as "whole self-leadership." Leadership in the church, in fact, should be noticeably unique. Observers of our leadership style—how we go about making decisions, how we run things, and how we talk—should have a keen sense that what we are up to is unlike any other type of leadership they have witnessed in the world. Why? Three things are at stake: the detectability of the Kingdom of God, the definition of the church, and our doctrine of God.

The church leader is charged with the detectability of the Kingdom of God, called both to work toward the expansion of the Kingdom of God and to testify to its manifestations in our midst. If we do not regularly point and say, "'Look! The Lamb of God!'" (John 1:36), then who will? The Kingdom of God is often difficult to see, especially when other kingdoms are hard at work to silence its voice or deny its authority. And the Kingdom of God is often mixed up with other kingdoms that appear very close to doing God's work but use this feigned activity to exploit others for private gain. Detecting the Kingdom of God here and now has always been the church's mandate. But the church's capacity to follow through with this commission has had inconsistent success. When dimensions and determinations of the Kingdom of God seem up for grabs, what will be our response? Will we remain silent, waiting for others to voice the gaps? Or will we take risks and make bold claims about the power of the Kingdom of God toward change and transformation?

How the church leads defines what the church is. Our leadership cannot be separated from the church's identity and how others perceive it. How people imagine the purpose and meaning of church will be determined, in part, by our leadership. As leaders and public theologians, we are frequently the first face of the church that people encounter. Before there is church as a building or church as a community, church is who we are and what we say. Our way of leading offers a definition of church that can either present a positive first impression or leave a bad taste in the mouths of those who sense fear and judgment, indecisiveness and obscurity, instead of confidence and hope and grace.

The way you lead also communicates a doctrine of God. The church leader is often someone's first encounter with God. In your leadership, you witness to who God is and how God is at work in the world. From how you lead, people will wonder about this God whom you profess and if they should look for another portrayal of God. Regardless of whether you lead from embedded theological commitments, observers assume that you do. They believe that you have a kind of "in" with God and that, somehow, your words and actions are derived from that special knowledge. We might even say that your leadership traits could be perceived as those *of* God. You are, in the eyes of many, a representative of God, an exceptional envoy who possesses insights about God that others are unable to know. In your leadership, who are you depicting God to be?

The fundamental definition of ecclesial integrity is that there is a clear correlation between theological commitments and leadership demeaner, that how representatives of the church lead can be directly connected to who they think God is. Otherwise, the church is no different than a business or a corporation. Why is integrity vital for theological leadership? Because it matters to God. We do not get to lead in the church without some serious reflection about who we think God is or without coming to terms with our own theological commitments. We do not get to claim God's activity, which miraculously supports our mission, without adequate arguments that demonstrate how we are able to make those claims. Leadership in the church might look different if we actually acknowledged that God had a stake in the matter.

Furthermore, integrity is the very premise of the relationship between faith and works. "You must be doers of the word and not only hearers who mislead themselves. Those who hear but don't do the word are like those who look at their faces in a mirror. They look at themselves, walk away, and immediately forget what they were like" (Jas 1:22-24). The author of James reminds us that works are indeed manifestations of faith. As such, your works are an embodiment of the principles of your faith. We might think that we can hide our true theological suppositions, and perhaps desire to do so, in leadership traits with which most can agree or that have a kind of ubiquity that makes them impossible to question. But such self-deception inevitably leads to a performative contradiction at best and duplicity at worst.

EMBODY

And I said to my body. Softly: "I want to be your friend." It took a long breath.
And replied "I have been waiting my whole life for this."

—Nayyirah Waheed

Re-embracing the incarnation is essential for church leadership going forward. God gave a body to God's presence in the world in Jesus that was previously experienced by word and theophany. We know God fully in Jesus as an incarnated body. This distinctive belief at the root of Christianity, that God took on human flesh, the human body, in Jesus Christ should be the primary animation for those of us called to carry on Jesus's ministry in the world. This foundational claim of Christianity should, therefore, be central to all we do. But is it? The church cannot do leadership in God's future without taking God's incarnation seriously. Yet our leadership in the church perpetuates a disembodied sense, both of church and of theology. As Isherwood and Stuart write, "The Christian faith tells us that redemption is brought through the incarnation of God."[3] To what extent,

---

3. Lisa Isherwood and Elizabeth Stuart, *Introducing Body Theology* (Cleveland, OH: Pilgrim, 1998), 32.

however, have Christian leaders accepted alternate avenues to secure redemption and, in particular, how is it that these avenues have nothing to do with the life, death, resurrection, or ascension of Jesus?

Belief in the incarnation—trust in the incarnation—makes Christianity distinct from other theologies and religions. Does our leadership in the church communicate this fundamental belief? It is a unique perspective, a remarkable claim, that God became human and, yet, we have allowed Christianity to devolve into doctrine and dogma devoid of flesh and blood. We hold up and encourage leadership that is only about the demonstration of certain skillsets that then become criteria for success. Absent is an insistence that successful leadership in the church should be evaluated based on the leader's theological integrity or the leader's ability to embody core theological commitments. As Amy P. McCullough writes, "To speak of embodiment is to reach for the collection of habitations and movements one acquires on the journey to a competent, meaning-making self."[4]

As a verb, *embody* assumes that leadership is first and foremost that which we do and is inseparable from who we are. Our capacity to compartmentalize our lives is not absent from how we choose to lead. We siphon off pieces of ourselves without ever realizing the toll that takes. We do so, and admirably so, toward protecting appropriate boundaries or thinking that ministry demands a controlled vulnerability. There is much truth in such endeavors. Boundaries are in place for your protection, as well as for those to whom you minister and with whom you do ministry. Embodiment disappears when those boundaries create a kind of rigidity that then precludes actual embodied reactions. Given some of our "rules" for doing ministry these days, no wonder there is critique of Jesus's response to Lazarus's death. That Jesus wept would seem, well, inappropriate. He is, after all, supposed to be the calming presence in the midst of grief and loss. Furthermore, embodiment purports that "the body is a social encounter, not

4. Amy P. McCollough, *Her Preaching Body* (Eugene, OR: Cascade, 2018), 162.

just a vessel for our hyper-individualism."[5] We do leadership in and for the sake of the church. The church, at its heart, is not a structure or programming, it is not an institution or a building—it is a community.

To some extent, ministry does necessitate certain limits to our vulnerability. The incarnation does not give us theological permission to air the entirety of our hurt or pain. No one needs to know how every aspect of our lives intersects with the gospel, especially when it is at the expense of present or past relationships. With whom we are vulnerable is, in some respects, an earned event, and it is an act of perceived trust. Unsolicited and poorly timed vulnerability only casts the vision on you. At the same time, as leaders in the church, we are keenly aware of how difficult it is to hide, even though we think we can. We imagine a kind of superhero ability toward self-restraint when it comes to congregational expectations and denominational exigencies. We assume that we can even hide behind said requirements without letting our true selves come through.

Of what are we afraid? Are we afraid of losing our callings or of not being liked? Are we afraid that our numbers cannot compete with the church down the road? Are we afraid that we will be looked over, passed over, or ignored because what we have is not shiny or innovative enough? Each of these questions gets to the very heart of the problem when the church adopts leadership models, characteristics, and terminology outside of its scripture, traditions, and theology. We abdicate the church's definitions of success and effectiveness to society's metrics of measurable and quantifiable data, when the truth is that embodied leadership can never be that prescribed.

Effectiveness and measurability are not traits found in the gospel. Time and time again, Jesus's ministry and the gospel itself resist these

---

5. Meghan O'Rourke, "The Shift Americans Must Make to Fight the Coronavirus," *The Atlantic*, March 12, 2020, https://www.theatlantic.com/ideas/archive/2020/03/we-need-isolate -ourselves-during-coronavirus-outbreak/607840/?utm_medium=social&utm_content=edit -promo&utm_campaign=the-atlantic&utm_term=2020-03-12T10%3A30%3A54&utm_so urce=facebook&fbclid=IwAR3tWFkpyd0N1W4sh1F38CT8NJ6jqXM2N9z4sMpOwq-9E _fAeNIi0tjROcc

kinds of quantifiers of accomplishment. "As Jesus left the temple, one of his disciples said to him, 'Teacher, look! What awesome stones and buildings!' Jesus responded, 'Do you see these enormous buildings? Not even one stone will be left upon another. All will be demolished'" (Mark 13:1). Yet, we keep on trying, buying into ways of doing leadership that are descriptive and not lived, that are skills-driven instead of theologically driven. Fleming Rutledge notes, "I read that a recent experiment in church growth and development did not achieve the expected 'outcome metrics.' If the mainline churches keep using language like this, church growth is doomed."[6] Leadership in the church is not a constellation of principles but an embodiment of God's presence in our midst.

MORE ABOUT EMBODIMENT

Never forget how wildly capable you are.

—Unknown

The first definition of *embody*, according to Merriam-Webster is: "to give a body to (a spirit): INCARNATE."[7] Synonyms of *embody* include: absorb, assimilate, co-opt, incorporate, and integrate. We might ask ourselves: Do we embody the incarnation in our ministry? Do we take seriously the meaning of *embody* in how we describe and execute our leadership? Do we regularly think about how we are embodying that which is at stake for our leadership? Do we merely describe our leadership, rather than give a body to it? These are the primary questions that this book seeks to answer. As McCullough writes, "Embodiment encircles the physical body and the living self, for how we live cannot be separated from the form by which we

---

6. Fleming Rutledge, @femingrut, Twitter, July 1, 2019.

7. "Embody," *Merriam-Webster Online Dictionary*, https://www.merriam-webster.com/dictionary/embody, accessed February 14, 2020.

live."[8] To believe in the incarnation is to believe in this truth: bodies matter to God. When bodies do not matter, when our very bodies do not matter, then we are not confessing fully that the Word became flesh. The truth is, for too many of us, there is an avid denial of body when it comes to our leadership. This is especially complicated by the fact that for many people, especially for women leaders in the church, their bodies have been the source of pain that is the result of sexism, misogyny, and objectification.

Our lack of embodiment in leadership in the church communicates a lack of integrity on the part of the church. In practice, the extent to which the church bases its faith on the incarnation only goes so far in our leadership. We put provisions in place, acting on the premise that some bodies are more acceptable as the image of God than others. We also place these conditions on ourselves, acting on the idea that our bodies are not enough to do the work of God, that only certain bodies are suitable to lead in God's church—and mostly those bodies are expected to conform to society's standards. These standards, of course, are neither reachable nor real. They do not take into account the truths of flesh and bone. Furthermore, they perpetuate the ways in which humanity classifies what it perceives to be good and acceptable in God's eyes. Thus, bodies have to be thin, attractive, white, young, clearly gendered, and able-bodied; as such, the church is then complicit in ageism, sexism, racism, heteronormativity, and ableism. This is what is at stake when we talk about embodiment and leadership in the church.

It is not enough anymore to celebrate inclusivity or milestones made on behalf of the church's openness to other kinds of bodies. Leaders need to lead "embodiedly" as a daily resistance to society's ongoing marginalization of the bodies of women, transgender and gender nonconforming bodies, disabled bodies, violated bodies, violenced bodies, and nonwhite bodies. For too long, the church has been complicit in what bodies it is willing to

---

8. McCollough, *Her Preaching Body*, 162.

accept to preach from its pulpits; to teach in its seminaries; and to serve from leadership positions held in synodical, judicatory, institutional, and sessional structures.

Embodiment counteracts tokenism. Embodiment chooses intention. Embodiment insists how leaders lead is truly an extension of the self. Embodiment demands that your body matters, even when the church dismisses your body. Embodiment is the correction when the church demands a dedication of bodies over and above any other profession in the form of a self-sacrifice suggested by the cross rather than of a self-care advocated by the incarnation. As such, embodiment is not a euphemism for behavior or acting out certain characteristics. Rather, embodiment is the essential category by which we describe ministry based on the incarnation. To embrace embodiment is to embrace change, not just for the sake of change or for a perceived benefit of disruption; rather, centering leadership in embodiment embraces the fact that bodies are unreliable. They can betray us. They disappoint us. When we realize this truth, then we begin to understand that the mind is no different. Theology, models of church leadership, ways of going about church, are in the mode of relying heavily on the mind—as if the mind can solve every issue that the body finds difficult.

Messiness and unpredictability are inherent to embodiment, which is likely why leadership in the church sets embodiment aside in favor of leadership agendas that rely on ideals and plans. However, this is not how embodiment works. If the church and its leaders were actually living into the identity as the embodied spirit of God in the world, then this would mean letting go of that which is most valued in society's definition of leadership. It would mean for the church's leaders to embrace vulnerability. It would mean a transformation from being market-driven to being spirit-driven, and it would mean moving from using strategic rhetoric to using soul-speech, from being policy-driven to being relationship-driven. It would mean moving from being manual-driven to being Bible-driven. It would mean giving up on competition and striving for distinctiveness—a distinctiveness in leadership that actually embodies what it believes theologically. Frailty, fragility, and finitude are not the desired traits to headline an institution, and yet that is how God chose to reveal God's very self. The church's redemption "could not be wished or just thought, even by God herself, she had to be enfleshed."[9]

Embodiment also suggests that experience is worthy of theological revelation, that theology "springs from" the body.[10] The church has exercised considerable effort in erasing theology that is born out of experience. After all, this is not a theology that is provable; nor is it a theology that can function as criteria for defending orthodoxy. It is no wonder, then, that when the New Testament was in the canonization process, claiming inspiration could not be a criterion for inclusion. But, as McCollough writes, "theology can no longer shroud us in the comforts of eternal absolutes."[11] Nor should theology any longer be our reason for eschewing our own embodied experiences.

The truth of the incarnation suggests, even demands, that wisdom is not found in the many answers set forth by leadership models but in the very bodies of those who have heard God's call and have responded, "Here I am" and thereby taking "I am" seriously, just as Job does: "then from my flesh I'll see God" (Job 19:26). And whereas the church's history has held up a male body as normative and as representative of leadership in the church, the church has had a poor track record when it comes to addressing sexual abuse in the church.

The church can stand as a counterpoint to the ways in which bodies are dismissed in so many diverse aspects of life. The church can also seek to correct how society only accepts certain bodies, especially the bodies wanted to represent the church. As Isherwood and Stuart note: "What

---

9.   Isherwood and Stuart, *Introducing Body Theology*, 32.

10.   Isherwood and Stuart, *Introducing Body Theology*, 33.

11.   Isherwood and Stuart, *Introducing Body Theology*, 39.

must be guarded against at all costs is the disappearance of the real, lived, laughing, suffering, birthing, and dying body underneath the philosophical and theological meaning it is called to bear. It would indeed be foolish to allow 'the body' to become a disembodied entity."[12]

When bodies are dismissed for not meeting the criteria of what they hold up, then how can they be "sites of resistance"?[13] To believe in the incarnation is to insist that the body is the locus of theological experience: "The body is integral to the self and a place from which individual, social, institutional, and political knowledge is revealed."[14]

What difference would it make for leadership in the church if the church "took seriously as Scripture surely does: that the privileged arena of divine disclosure is the human body."[15] We have conveniently forgotten that scripture itself witnesses to God's revelation to, and in, bodies. God, and every way God acts, is experienced through bodies. The entirety of the biblical witness testifies to manifestations of God landing on, and working through, actual bodies.

WHAT YOU CAN EXPECT

Beware of turning into the enemy you most fear. All it takes is to lash out violently at someone who has done you some grievous harm, proclaiming that only your pain matters in this world. More than against that person's body, you will then, at that moment, be committing a crime against your own imagination.

—Ariel Dorfman

What follows is five keys that embody theological integrity in leadership. Included in each chapter is a section for further reflection that offers

---

12. Isherwood and Stuart, *Introducing Body Theology*, 151

13. Isherwood and Stuart, *Introducing Body Theology*, 100.

14. McCollough, *Her Preaching Body*, 13.

15. Luke Timothy Johnson, *The Revelatory Body: Theology as Inductive Art* (Grand Rapids: Eerdmans, 2015), ix.

questions and exercises for both individual and group attention. These five keys are born out of the primary activities of the *paraclete* in John's Gospel that are then embodied in the discipleship of five women characters in John. These five bodies bear witness to God's revelation in Jesus Christ. When leaders in the church imagine themselves as paracletes, then it is these five keys that can be manifested in how they lead: accompaniment, attentiveness, authenticity, abundance, and advocacy. Each chapter begins with *observations* that present fundamental assumptions of the key being discussed, particularly against the backdrop of contemporary leadership discussions. Next, each chapter has a section devoted to *theological premises*, which situates the chapter's key principle in the wider framework of God's nature and activity, especially on the foundation of the incarnation. The third section of each chapter is a discussion of where we see that chapter's key at work specifically in the presence and portrait of the *paraclete*. The fourth section examines how a *woman character* in the Gospel of John embodies the suggested key component of leadership. Finally, each chapter concludes with *further reflection* that provides a list of exercises, questions, and readings for additional consideration about how to imagine embodying these five key aspects of the *paraclete* in our leadership.

How we engage with scripture for the sake of embodied leadership is critical. As Luke Timothy Johnson writes, "Scripture's use of body language urges us to think more constructively about what Scripture suggests about human bodies generally in connection with knowing the world and knowing God—that is, what it has to say about human bodies as medium of revelation."[16] John's Gospel takes seriously the nature of these embodied encounters between Jesus and the five women we will meet in the Fourth Gospel. Their experiences of Jesus lead to their own embodiment of who Jesus is. Johnson notes: "Scripture has been reduced to a storehouse of propositions from which deductions can be made, rather than a collection

---

16. Johnson, *The Revelatory Body*, 53.

of witnesses that also enable believers to witness to God's work and glorify God's presence among them."[17] These five women in John's Gospel—the mother of Jesus, the Samaritan woman at the well, Martha, Mary, and Mary Magdalene—witness to what embodying the *paraclete* looks like. The discussions of these extraordinary women are meant to illustrate the key at work in each woman's character, thus providing a textual study for individuals or groups working through the material provided in this book.

"Authentic faith is more than a matter of right belief; it is the response of human beings in trust and obedience to the one whom Scripture designates as the Living God, in contrast to the dead idols that are constructed by humans as projections of their own desires."[18] Leadership in the church should strive for this kind of authentic faith; the church should strive for leadership that does not subscribe to human constructions of leadership and human attempts to fit a Spirit-filled church into a human-made ideal, but leadership that looks for the living God at work in the church, for the sake of the world. A focus on embodiment is not the only way to imagine leadership in the church, but it can be a significant means to stay true to the full promise of the incarnation in how we lead. Leadership in the church is distinct when it witnesses to a present God, when how we lead is not governed by a set of principles but is born out of encounters with the living God in Jesus Christ.

Embodiment also means that we make a shift from talking about *leadership* to talking about *leaders*. Leadership is an abstract concept that can easily take on characteristics all on its own without ever being connected to incarnated realities and truths. It is unhelpful to talk about leadership in the third person. Once we use the word *leader*, then we can attach it to a person. That is, "What kind of leader is she?" is a different question altogether than "What kind of leadership traits does she have?"

---

17. Johnson, *The Revelatory Body*, 38.

18. Johnson, *The Revelatory Body*, 1.

Trust in the incarnation means that Jesus literally incorporated and incarnated the descriptors we use for God. The theological vocabulary we like to use when it comes to denominational identity means nothing if then not acted out, performed, and experienced. For example, consider the word *grace* and its pandenominational use in the church. Much effort is extended toward defining *grace* without reaching any consensus. *Grace* is mercy, love, and steadfastness—to name only a few words used to define *grace*. This makes sense because we are talking about God's grace after all, and to insist on a particular or singular descriptor for *grace* would then lead to making a similar assumption about what might be possible about God.

Of course, *grace* is used extensively in the New Testament, albeit with differing definitions at work, depending on the author. The use of *grace* in the Gospel of John, however, illustrates the move from a third-person reference or definition to a first-person embodiment. In the Gospel of John, the word *grace* is used only four times and is only used in the prologue (John 1:1-18 [vv. 14, 16, and 17]). The prologue presents essential theological themes that are then unpacked in the rest of the narrative; in particular, theological themes related to Jesus's origin and Jesus's identity. This cosmic birth story, if you will, is told in a third-person discourse, laying out certain principles that are both assumed and demonstrated or validated as the story progresses. Because of the fundamental theological premise of the incarnation, however, these theological statements cannot be left in the abstract as merely descriptive of God's revelation in Jesus. The Word becoming flesh (John 1:14) means that God assumed a new identity. God is now ontologically different, and that makes a difference for how God then reveals God's very self.

As a result, what follows after the prologue is a set of claims made about God, and most directly, claims that the Word from the beginning is now flesh, is enfleshed and embodied. From John 1:19 onward, there is a fundamental shift in how the narrative even feels. The tone is altogether different, going from explanation to incarnation.

Once the Gospel establishes that the Word has become flesh, therefore, the rest of the Gospel narrates not what grace means but how grace is experienced. The Gospel of John manifests a kind of tension between principles and praxis. *Grace* is no longer defined because it is now definitively among us, abiding with us. After John 1:17, the word *grace* never again appears in the entire Gospel of John because grace is no longer a concept but an experience. As such, having a relationship with Jesus is grace in and of itself, and as soon as we go down the road of trying to quantify or codify this relationship, we have missed the point altogether.

Our tendency as church leaders is to carry on as if sound theological credibility were essential to our credibility, when in fact, systematic theology is oxymoronic idolatry.[19] The systemization of theology is an act of idolatry because we have privileged the categorization of God over the knowing of God. But when the incarnation is front and center as a Christian leader, then we begin to realize that what we do and who we are must be indistinguishable.

We have a penchant to equate scripture with the living God, when scripture actually invites witness to the living God. This changes our hermeneutical approach. The five women characters we will encounter embody who Jesus is as a leader. As Johnson writes in *The Revelatory Body*, "From the beginning, Scripture functioned as a participation in the process of revelation."[20] These characters embody experiences of revelation. It is up to leaders in the church to commit to embodiment and to lead embodiedly, otherwise "theology remains a discipline concerned above all

---

19. Johnson, *The Revelatory Body*, 12.

20. Johnson, *The Revelatory Body*, 3.

with texts and propositions based in the past, rather than discernment of the work of the Living God in the present."[21]

YOUR STORY

Before you continue, take this moment to reflect about yourself as a leader. What characteristics immediately come to mind, and why? Are these traits you have determined for yourself or how others have described you? Have they been ascertained by certain leadership analyses or tests? Are they characteristics outlined in a book that you were told to read? Are you able to connect these characteristics to central aspects of who you are and who you know yourself to be? Or are these qualities more surface descriptions of what you can do or of kinds of tasks you are able to accomplish? More importantly, can you associate these leadership skills or characteristics directly to your theological commitments? Do any of them actually originate from a belief in God that you hold dear? Or do you sense a disconnect and a feeling of disembodied leadership, either because you are acting based on others' expectations or because you cannot, as hard as you try, attach these attributes to what is at stake for you theologically?

Ask yourself these questions: Why are you reading this book? What do you feel is lacking in your leadership? It is important to be able to name your motivations for wanting to dedicate your time and efforts to your identity as a leader so that you can have a sense of change or transformation after doing the work. Some additional questions that will be important to ask are: What is the core reason for picking up this book? Do you have an awareness of some discomfort or dis-ease? Do you have the impression that your leadership is in need of either a reboot or a renewal? What and where are the points of perceived change? Or perhaps you may

---

21. Johnson, *The Revelatory Body*, 15.

be sensing that there has been an event, or a series of events or issues, that has intimated a need for a kind of reorientation in who you are as a leader. Often, such an identified event is a crisis moment, when your leadership has been questioned, or when the structures on which you have relied are no longer valid. The COVID-19 pandemic is one example of the unprecedented leadership challenges that result from crisis moments.

The following are some axles of transformation, among which you might be able to trace an advancement in how you think about your leadership and how you want to lead. If none of these axles resonate with you, document your own desires for movement:

Uncertainty—Confidence

Compartmentalization—Connection

Trapped—Liberated

Feeling silenced—Finding Your Voice

Disembodied—Embodiment

Fear—Joy

Lack of distinctiveness—Potential Realized

Tracking movement in your feelings about, and perceptions of, your leadership will result in tangible change. When change is tangible, then it can be embodied in how you go about leading. You will feel different, and others will sense that difference. In other words, in order to move toward embodied change, you have to embody that transformation along the way. There needs to be actual moments and experiences in which you sense and know in your entire being that something has changed. That is what it means to be embodied and to commit to embodiment.

As noted above, the five chapters set out five keys of Christian leadership: accompaniment, attentiveness, authenticity, abundance, and advocacy. While these biblical descriptors are critical for the Christian leader, they also provide an operating hermeneutic, both to bring to scripture and to make sense of the world. That is, the Christian leader actively looks for ways in which these manifestations of God's being are present in the biblical witness and in the living witness of God's people here and now; then Christian leaders seek to embody these very principles in every aspect of leading the Christian communities to which they are called.

ACCOMPANIMENT

Abide with Me

Abide with me; fast falls the eventide;

The darkness deepens; Lord, with me abide;

When other helpers fail and comforts flee,

Help of the helpless, oh, abide with me.

Swift to its close ebbs out life's little day;

Earth's joys grow dim, its glories pass away;

Change and decay in all around I see—

O Thou who changest not, abide with me.

I need Thy presence every passing hour;

What but Thy grace can foil the tempter's pow'r?

Who, like Thyself, my guide and stay can be?

Through cloud and sunshine, Lord, abide with me.

I fear no foe, with Thee at hand to bless;

Ills have no weight, and tears no bitterness;

Where is death's sting? Where, grave, thy victory?

I triumph still, if Thou abide with me.

Hold Thou Thy cross before my closing eyes;

Shine through the gloom and point me to the skies;

Heav'n's morning breaks, and earth's vain shadows flee;

In life, in death, O Lord, abide with me.[1]

—Henry Francis Lyte

---

1. Hymn text by Henry Francis Lyte, written in 1847.

Chapter One
ACCOMPANIMENT

OBSERVATIONS

Pay attention to your patterns. The ways you learned to survive may not be
the ways you want to continue to live. Shift and heal.

—Unknown

Jesus's first act as a leader was to accompany his disciples. When we re-
call that the fundamental meaning of *paraclete* is the one who is called
to be alongside others, we realize that the first principle of Christian leadership is not a characteristic but a way of being. When Jesus says to his
disciples, "I am sending you another *paraclete*," it is not only a statement
about his own ministry, but it also indicates the principle reality of what a
leader who claims to be Christian then does. The promise of the *paraclete*
solidifies the fact that essential to Christian leadership is not a set of skills
but being a consistent presence.

Being a leader with a "Christian" identity demands that there are observable and distinctive ways of being and, therefore, of leading, by making intentional connections to Jesus's own embodiment of leadership. It is
not enough to assume that your faith is a sufficient category by which to

define "Christian" when you identify as a Christian leader. It is incumbent upon us to strive for ways to articulate what it means to be a Christian leader; that is, what it means to be a leader who embodies the very leadership of Jesus. The word *Christian* was never meant to be merely adjectival. *Christian* signals a relationship with Jesus, without which we are, and would be, like any other leader.

This is challenging work. The human propensity to make comparisons, especially in ways able to be measured, is not going away anytime soon. As ministry is inherently an activity of delayed gratification, the ability to chart *any* indicators of supposed success is a temptation that is terribly hard to resist. And yet, to what extent has the church abandoned theological integrity for institutional survival? The sky may be falling, the church may be dying, but the canary in the coal mine has never been the church's inability to adapt. It has been, and will likely continue to be, a cry from the cross. When our calling to reimagine leadership in the church is a return to the premises and promises of the gospel, we should expect resistance. We will appear traditionalist, unable to innovate, or unrealistic in our ideal of recovering the past glory of the church. But the gospel, as the promise of the presence of God, has always been a forward-looking truth.

As noted above, much talk about leadership in the church these days is about leadership characteristics or traits that are effective for success, but rarely do we come across a discussion about whether these traits actually embody who you are or who God has called you to be. Identifying markers of Jesus's leadership are manifestations of being and identity, not skills to learn, characteristics for which to strive, or techniques to apply. Fundamentally, Christian leadership is not a set of prescribed descriptors but rather an embodiment of our relationship with Jesus Christ, with God, and with the Holy Spirit.

When the incarnation becomes the foundational premise for leadership in the church, relationship is then at the core of the church leader. The very idea of incarnation assumes that relationship will be absolutely central. Accompaniment is the embodiment of relationship. It is no wonder, however, that the church has a tendency to shy away from this inherent aspect of the church's calling. To hold relationship as the hallmark of leadership ultimately leads to less-than-controlled realities and, more often than not, out-of-control situations. Relationships are innately instable and unpredictable. They eschew prediction and demand flexibility. None of these resulting qualities are necessarily those that most leaders are willing to profess.

If you are reading this book, then you have sensed this disconnection of relationship and leadership and want to do something about it. Leading with integrity, regardless of venue, is not for the faint of heart. An integrated leader is often met with suspicion and often seen as one having it just "too much together." Integrated leaders lead from their truth, and few people have the courage to figure out and name the truth about themselves. It is easier to adopt acceptable characteristics and mainstream measures and adapt to trends rather than engage in the hard work of self-reflection and self-interpretation. Without the church's leaders' willingness to take a long look at themselves and admit where they have given up on theology for the sake of productivity, the church will blend into its surroundings; it will mold itself to the latest fads and be almost indiscernible as the embodiment of God's love in the world. The church would do well to hear once again and take to heart Paul's admonishment of the Galatians: "I'm amazed that you are so quickly deserting the one who called you by the grace of Christ to follow another gospel" (Gal 1:6).

THEOLOGICAL PREMISE

We are what we repeatedly do. Excellence, therefore, is not an act, but a habit.

—Aristotle

Committing to leadership in the church that relies on scripture is risky. After all, what could the Bible possibly offer the church for imagination in leadership in this day and age? From Moses to the kings to the prophets to religious representatives, none are exempt from critique. Such witness does not leave us very eager to explore the leadership elements of these persons charged with commanding the people of God. But central in scripture is the importance of accompaniment as a designation of God's very identity. God has been committed to accompaniment all along, as we see in Leviticus: "I will walk around among you; I will be your God, and you will be my people" (26:12). Exodus narrates the construction of the tent or tabernacle for the ark of the covenant so that God can indeed go wherever God's people go. God's accompaniment is a primary theological theme in the book of Numbers, as the Israelites travel from Mount Sinai to the promised land:

> They marched from the LORD's mountain for three days. The LORD's chest containing the covenant [ark of the covenant] marched ahead of them for three days to look for a resting place for them. Now the LORD's cloud was over them by day when they marched from the camp. When the chest set out, Moses would say, "Arise, LORD, let your enemies scatter, and those who hate you flee." When it rested, he would say, "Return, LORD of the ten thousand thousands of Israel." (Num 10:33-36)

God's dwelling with God's people is especially noted when God's presence is called into question. God promises to accompany God's people no matter where they are. As a leader in the church, another way to imagine accompaniment, therefore, is this kind of promised divine dwelling.

The Fourth Evangelist recognizes that in Jesus, God is once again tabernacling with us. John's Gospel, just as with the Synoptic Gospels, addresses the theological crisis of the destruction of the temple and the razing of Jerusalem by the Roman Empire in 70 CE. Without the temple, the presence of God was again uncertain. Each of the four evangelists responds to this defining moment in very distinct ways, presenting portraits of Jesus that both offer their interpretations of the person and work of Christ and seek to address this apparent absence of God. For John, Jesus is both the presence of God and is God. The particularity and inseparableness of these two promises lie at the very heart of Jesus-as-leader in the Gospel of John. Jesus's presence and Jesus's identity, Jesus's accompaniment and Jesus's being, are distinctive and yet indissoluble. God's being, to be present, is God's very nature. For God to dwell among us is central to who God is. God cannot NOT be with us. It is an expression of God's very heart.

Additional evidence of this truth of God is the temple incident in John. In the Fourth Gospel, the temple incident—that is, the story of Jesus entering the temple, turning over its tables, and verbally critiquing temple practices—is moved from the end of Jesus's public ministry to the very beginning of Jesus's public ministry (John 2:13-22). Whereas in Matthew, Mark, and Luke, the temple incident is the provocation for Jesus's arrest, in John, the impetus is raising Lazarus from the dead. The temple incident, therefore, has a very different function in the Gospel of John compared to the Gospels of Matthew, Mark, and Luke. For John, the temple incident is an affirmation of Jesus's true identity, as the "Word was God" (John 1:1). In John, the critique lodged against the temple is not "Stop making my Father's house a den of robbers" (see Matt 21:12-17; Mark 11:15-19; Luke 19:45-48), with an assumed motive to call out some kind of corruption, but "Stop making my Father's house a marketplace" (John 2:13-16). However, the temple as a marketplace was essential for the survival of the Jewish religious sacrificial system. The pilgrimage festivals—Passover, Weeks, and Booths—necessitated exchanges for proper sacrifices, typically grains traded for the required animal sacrifice. Basically, Jesus says that the entire system is unnecessary in part because he is and will be the ultimate sacrifice, the sacrificial lamb (John 1:29), and also because the temple is no longer the location of God. God is present in Jesus, the I AM, the Word made flesh.

The function of the temple incident in John, stating Jesus's true identity, is reinforced by the exchange between Jesus and the temple authorities. Jesus says to them: "Destroy this temple and in three days I will raise it up" (John 2:19). The temple priests respond: "It took forty-six years to build this temple, and you will raise it up in three days?" (v. 20). John's narrator then clarifies Jesus's statement: "But the temple Jesus was talking about was his body" (v. 21). For the Fourth Evangelist, it is critical for us to know immediately the true identity of Jesus. Jesus is God and, therefore, Jesus's presence among us is a given.

In chapter 4, there is similar affirmation of Jesus's identity during the conversation between Jesus and the woman at the well. When the Samaritan woman inquires of Jesus where the proper place to worship might be, when the Jews worshiped God in the temple in Jerusalem and the Samaritans offered their worship of God in the temple on Mount Gerazim, Jesus answers: "neither on this mountain nor in Jerusalem" (v. 21). In other words, God's presence is no longer in the temple but in the body of Jesus Christ. God's presence is no longer a building but a person. God's presence is God's being.

John 1:14 asserts that the Word became flesh and dwelt among us or lived among us. The word translated as "lived/dwelt" is *skenaō*, which means "to tent or to tabernacle." God, in Jesus, is once again tenting among God's people, but in Jesus, God is not only going where they go but also is who they are. In other words, God's accompaniment cannot be separated from God's identity; the dwelling of God is not just something that God does but who God desires, even has to be. We find this same promise in the book of Revelation, the only other New Testament book in the New Testament besides the Gospel of John that uses the term *skenaō*. The final theological theme and image in Revelation is God's city, the New Jerusalem, coming down so that once again God can dwell with God's people:

> Then I saw a new heaven and a new earth, for the former heaven and the former earth had passed away, and the sea was no more. I saw the holy city, New Jerusalem, coming down out of heaven from God, made ready as a bride beautifully dressed for her husband. I heard a loud voice from the throne say, "Look! God's dwelling [tabernacle] is here with humankind. He will dwell [tabernacle] with them, and they will be his peoples. God himself will be with them as their God. He will wipe away every tear from their eyes. Death will be no more. There will be no mourning, crying, or pain anymore, for the former things have passed away." (Rev 21:1-4)

This promise would have been especially critical for the churches to whom the book of Revelation was written, which were experiencing internal ecclesial challenges and even more dire pressures and persecutions from the outside world, particularly from the power of the Roman Empire. One of the primary themes of apocalyptic literature is to reiterate God's presence and power in the midst of what seems to be God's absence and ineffective sovereignty.

What difference does this scriptural narration make for how we think about accompaniment as a leader in the church? We begin to realize that accompaniment is not just a characteristic of God's leadership or of Jesus's leadership, but that accompaniment is who God is, who Jesus is. Accompaniment, therefore, is not a skill one lists on a resumé for a job in church leadership but is that by which one embodies who God has been as God, as the Word made flesh, and, now, as the promise of the *paraclete*.

Accompaniment intimates a distinctive kind of authority. The promise of God's accompaniment is reiterated in those times when God's presence appears to be most needed or most questioned. This suggests that accompaniment becomes necessary especially in periods of vulnerability, fear, and uncertainty. As a result, the kind of accompaniment in which the church leader engages is not a mere ministry of presence but a true sense of an embodied divine pathos. It is a kind of accompaniment that is not simply about being present but is about recognizing that this moment might indicate a theological crisis: Is God really here?

THE PROMISE OF THE PARACLETE

I used to think that the worst thing in life was to end up alone. It's not. The worst thing in life is to end up with people who make you feel alone.

—Robin Williams

"I am sending you another *paraclete*" recalls Jesus's accompaniment of his disciples during the course of his public ministry and also looks forward to the necessity of this accompaniment going forward. Here, Jesus's words remember the entirety of his ministry in this one word, *paraclete*. Because Jesus had already been the *paraclete*, then this image, this promise, this metaphor, is the lens through which to interpret his three-year ministry.

This accompaniment manifests itself in a variety of ways throughout the rest of the Farewell Discourse. First, the *paraclete* abides: "You know him, because he abides with you, and he will be in you" (John 14:17 NRSV). Next, "the Companion, the Holy Spirit, whom the Father will send in my name, will teach you everything and remind you of everything I told you" (John 14:26). The *paraclete* witnesses for the sake of Jesus: "When the Companion comes, whom I will send from the Father—the Spirit of Truth who proceeds from the Father—he will testify about me" (John 15:26). Jesus also notes that when he leaves, he will then send the *paraclete*: "When he comes, he will show the world it was wrong about sin, righteousness, and judgment. He will show the world it was wrong about sin because they don't believe in me. He will show the world it was wrong about righteousness because I'm going to the Father and you won't see me anymore. He will show the world it was wrong about judgment because this world's ruler stands condemned" (John 16:8-11). This accompaniment is primarily because of the weight the disciples will be asked to carry. It is an accompaniment for the sake of pastoral presence and comfort: "I have much more to say to you, but you can't handle it now. However, when the Spirit of Truth comes, he will guide you in all truth. He won't speak on his own, but will say whatever he hears and will proclaim to you what is to come. He will glorify me, because he will take what is mine and proclaim it to you. Everything that the Father has is mine. That's why I said that the Spirit takes what is mine and will proclaim it to you" (John 16:12-15). And yet, the first reference to the *paraclete* does not articulate these specific activities that the Spirit will carry out but emphasizes the *paraclete*'s presence, being, companionship, and the walking alongside others.

We noted above that Jesus provides a retrospective description of the kind of leader he has been when he promises the disciples that God will send "another Companion" (John 14:16). Jesus himself has already been the *paraclete* for his disciples. At the same time, John casts the conceptual net a little wider by presenting accompaniment also as abiding. In other words, before the introduction of *paraclete* in the Farewell Discourse, Jesus has been the *paraclete* for his disciples through the primary expression of *abide*, or in Greek, *menō*.

Used over forty times in the Gospel of John, *menō*, which is translated as "abide, remain, stay, continue," is the central word that describes the relationship the believer has with Jesus. To abide is to believe, is to be in an intimate relationship with both Jesus and God. To abide is to come into the presence of God, the presence of Jesus. Relationship with Jesus is both initiated and confirmed in abiding. Accompaniment is an invitation and commitment to relationship. If we track the references of the use of *abiding* prior to the *paraclete* and the Farewell Discourse, abiding leads to believing, which then ends in relationship that brings about abundant life (John 10:10).

The first use of *menō* occurs in the calling of the disciples:

> The next day John was standing again with two of his disciples. When he saw Jesus walking along he said, "Look! The Lamb of God!" The two disciples heard what he said, and they followed Jesus. When Jesus turned and saw them following, he asked, "What are you looking for?" They said, "Rabbi (which is translated *Teacher*), where are you staying?" He replied, "Come and see." So they went and saw where he was staying [*menō*], and they remained [*menō*] with him that day. It was about four o'clock in the afternoon. One of the two disciples who heard what John said and followed Jesus was Andrew, the brother of Simon Peter. He first found his brother Simon and said to him, "We have found the Messiah" (which is translated *Christ*). He led him to Jesus. Jesus looked at him and said, "You are Simon, son of John. You will be called Cephas" (which is translated *Peter*). (John 1:35-42)

Abiding with Jesus leads to affirmation of Jesus's identity, "We have found the Messiah," and this revelation of Jesus as the Christ then results in the invitation to others to abide with Jesus. Jesus's identity cannot be fully known unless you yourself abide with Jesus. To abide with Jesus is the promise of Jesus's accompaniment. Abiding indicates believing in, and relationship with, Jesus. The vine-and-branches metaphor in the Farewell Discourse is the last "I AM" statement in John with a predicate nominative, "I AM the vine," and the last affirmation from Jesus about the mutual abiding between him and his disciples, "Remain (abide/*menō*) in me, and I will remain in you" (John 15:4). After the vine and the branches, the only two other occurrences of abide/*menō* after the Farewell Discourse (the last occurrence in 15:16) are in 19:31 and 21:22-23, neither of which indicates a relational connection. That is, once the promise of the *paraclete* is given, the *paraclete* takes over the accompaniment. The *paraclete* embodies abiding. "This Companion is the Spirit of Truth, whom the world can't receive because it neither sees him nor recognizes him. You know him, because he lives [*menō*] with you and will be with you" (John 14:17).

The theological promise of accompaniment is both God's promise and is also filled with promise for the Christian leader. Accompaniment, therefore, is not simply something that we do, but it embodies who Jesus was for his disciples and then who the Holy Spirit was, and is, for believers, both then and now. We embody accompaniment, commit to accompaniment, and do accompaniment because this was who Jesus was as a leader. Accompaniment is central to Jesus's mission and vision, in part because accompaniment is born out of relationship and thus also maintains relationship. Beginning and encouraging relationship, therefore, appears to be a hallmark for how Jesus understood his ministry and himself as one who leads.

The accompaniment of the *paraclete* is literally, or narratively, embodied in the Farewell Discourse. The discourses about the Holy Spirit are not localized into one chapter or section as a single presentation. Rather, that which the *paraclete* will do, what Jesus has already done, is interspersed throughout the Farewell Discourse, and thus experienced by the disciples, in chapter 14 (14:8-17, 25-27), chapter 15 (15:26-27), and chapter 16 (16:4b-11). In other words, the Farewell Discourse's narrative mode underscores the theological claim of the *paraclete*'s presence. The promise of the *paraclete* as one who accompanies is not just something to know but something to be felt and experienced, through the hearing and reading of the Farewell Discourse itself.

Accompaniment is also who the disciples are for each other. Another term representing accompaniment is the word *friend*: "I don't call you servants any longer ... I call you friends" (John 15:15). We might assume that the concept of "friend" does not allow for a kind of necessary autonomy in leadership, especially when it comes to making hard decisions or to inevitable confrontation. In doing so, however, we will not have taken into account the understanding of friendship in the ancient world. Friendship was not a mere expression of affection or an emotional construction but intimated social responsibilities and assumed a bond that demanded values, virtues, and obligations.[2]

By using the word *friend* between the first reference to the *paraclete* in John (14:8-17, 25-27) and the second reference (15:26-27), Jesus suggests that there is an essential mutuality in accompaniment; that the one who accompanies needs the ones being accompanied, just as the one needs the accompanier. Jesus indicates an inherent reciprocity in accompanying by removing hierarchy—a hierarchy that the church has embedded into its own leadership models and which the church has implemented without much thought. To use the word *leader* fundamentally implies that there are followers. As such, it cannot be the only term the church uses to define how its leaders operate.

We tend to get nervous about these kinds of equilateral leadership designs. We are afraid to lose our own power, we are fearful of what might happen if power gets into the wrong hands, and we are especially anxious when we have to come face-to-face with our own privilege. We assume that if power is too evenly distributed, then it will result in a lack of direction and focus, or result in a lack of mission and vision. Yet, a careful reading of the description of the accompaniment of the *paraclete* in John yields a helpful corrective to such fears. We discover that this accompanier will testify to the Truth (John 15:26-27), show the world it was wrong about sin, righteousness, and judgment (16:8), guide and teach (16:13), and speak whatever is heard (16:13). In fact, one of the primary characteristics of friendship is boldness of speech and action. The Gospel of John references *parresia* ("openly," "boldly") more than any other New Testament book (7:4, 13, 26; 10:24; 11:14, 54; 16:25, 29; 18:20). Friendship, as it turns out, is not for the faint of heart. Accompaniment is not simply having someone beside you. Accompaniment is not a mere ministry of presence. Accompaniment means active and assertive abiding—an abiding

2. Gail R. O'Day, "Jesus as Friend in the Gospel of John," *Interpretation: A Journal of Bible and Theology* (vol 58, issue 2, April 1, 2004): 144–57.

that enters into places of fear and discomfort, uncertainty, and troubled hearts, and speaks the truth freely.

THE MOTHER OF JESUS

The only clear line I draw these days is this: when my religion tries to come between me and my neighbor, I will choose my neighbor...
Jesus never commanded me to love my religion.

—Barbara Brown Taylor

Mary, the mother of Jesus, is the character in John who most clearly embodies *Key One: Accompaniment*. In John's Gospel, Jesus's mother appears only twice. First, Mary is present at the wedding at Cana (John 2:1-11), which was Jesus's first public act of ministry in the Fourth Gospel; and second, she is present at the foot of the cross, along with the beloved disciple (John 19:26-27). Jesus's mother brackets his entire ministry. Such narrative *inclusio* communicates accompaniment. Mary has been there all along, of course before turning water into wine, but specifically, Mary is the one who abides with Jesus and accompanies Jesus during his entire ministry. No other character accompanies Jesus like she does in the Gospel of John. Certainly, the disciples accompany Jesus, but none is present at the cross except the beloved disciple, who was first introduced in John 13:23, and his mother. Because of his mother, Jesus knows what it is like to be accompanied, which then enables Jesus to embody the same.

In the example of Mary, we can see other features of the Christian leader as one who accompanies. First, embodying accompaniment means being present at critical moments, as well as being present in the day-to-day rhythms of life. Mary is there at Jesus's first miracle, the first sign, the first act that will expose him, bring him out into the open, and after which there is no going back. She is present in his ultimate exposure on the cross, in his unspeakable suffering, and when Jesus takes his last breath. Embodying accompaniment recognizes these places and spaces of vulnerability, fear, and pain; it means recognizing the poignancy of the moment, the pathos of the moment, and your own role in and responsibility for that moment. In other words, Mary accompanies Jesus in his most acute instances of vulnerability. She sees in these moments the absolute necessity of her presence, of her abiding. This is more than being a compassionate leader or a heart-felt leader. It is a total embodiment of the other's vulnerability and then entering into that space. Embodying accompaniment is true empathy.

Second, embodying accompaniment means encouragement of the other's God-given potential, but even more so, it means naming *where* God needs someone to be and *who* God needs someone to be. The sum of the Farewell Discourse in the Gospel of John is Jesus embodying this very aspect of accompaniment. As Jesus prepares for his impending arrest, he knows that the hour has come for the end of his ministry and the end of the incarnation, and he is specific about what he needs his disciples to do and who he needs them to be in his absence. And so, Jesus tells his disciples to love one another (John 13:31-35), tells them to bear much fruit (John 15:1-17), and sends them into the world (17:18; cf., 20:23). These "commandments" of Jesus are all different expressions of one mission: to be the I AM in the world when Jesus cannot be. The entire presentation of discipleship in the Gospel of John rests on a principle of accompaniment, to accompany the world as the disciples themselves were accompanied by Jesus.

Without Jesus's mother embodying accompaniment as encouragement, at least according to John, Jesus's public ministry would never have gotten off the ground. At the wedding at Cana, when the wine runs out, Jesus's mother notes the wedding faux pas to her son. Jesus's response is not a dismissal of her but an inability, at least in that moment, to recognize that he has the power to do something to change the situation. As a result, Jesus's mother tells the chief steward, "Do whatever he tells you" (John 2:5). Jesus offers two commands, both of which are obeyed, and the result is a miracle of abundance: "Jesus said to them, 'Fill the jars with water,' and they filled them to the brim. Then he told them, 'Now draw some from them and take it to the headwaiter,' and they did" (John 2:7-8). The six jars, each holding twenty to thirty gallons of water, are replaced with that same amount of premium wine and filled to the brim. In the Gospels of Matthew, Mark, and Luke, Jesus's empowerment for his public ministry comes from his baptism and his ability to resist Satan's temptations in the wilderness. In John, Jesus's baptism is downplayed, and the temptation in the wilderness is omitted. Rather, Jesus is emboldened to take the first step into his public ministry, to take the first step into embodying his own identity, by his mother's accompaniment, by her encouragement, and by her ability to see and identify his power. It is Mary's accompaniment that makes it possible for Jesus's ministry to get off the ground.

Jesus's mother's words, "do whatever he tells you," have a kind of self-fulfilling prophecy as the narrative unfolds. For the people who encounter Jesus and who follow his instructions just as his mother had set forth, life and relationship follow. Both the man who had been ill for thirty-eight years (in John 5) and the man who had been blind since birth (in John 9) obey Jesus's commands. To the first, Jesus commands: "'Get up! Pick up your mat and walk'" (5:8) and the man is immediately healed and able to walk. To the second man, Jesus commands: "'Go, wash in the pool of Siloam' (this word means *sent*)" (John 9:7), and the blind man is able to see. But more so, both men are reconnected to their communities and restored to their relationships. In other words, accompaniment as embodiment of encouragement is for the sake of much more than a quick fix, a doable solution, or a problem's immediate reversal. It is for the sake of life and relationship, and for the sake of then embodying the joy and wonder of that relationship in the world. That is, accompaniment encourages accompaniment. You cannot imagine accompanying, or know how to accompany another, without being accompanied yourself.

FURTHER REFLECTION

It is difficult to find happiness within oneself,
but it is impossible to find it anywhere else.

—Arthur Schopenhauer

Below are some exercises and questions that can be used both individually and communally to reflect about accompaniment as a key toward embodying Jesus's integrity as a leader.

1. Who can you identify as accompaniers in your life? Who have been your *paraclete*s? How do you know that these people have been more than mentors or coaches? Is there someone who would be the *paraclete* you need here and now, whom you could approach and ask to accompany you?

_____

_____

_____

_____

_____

_____

_____

_____

_____

_____

_____

2. Where, when, and for whom have you been a *paraclete*? Are you able to access how that experience felt and name some specific descriptors? What were you asked to do? How might you tap into that feeling once again, so that you have a good sense of what accompaniment feels like? And what it feels like in your body?

_____

_____

_____

_____

_____

_____

_____

_____

_____

_____

_____

_____

_____

_____

3. Reflect on the following reading. The metaphors we use to make sense of how we live embodied lives suggest key aspects of how we make connections among who we are, what we do, how we live, and how we lead.

Following the Thread

There's a thread you follow. It goes among

things that change. But it doesn't change.

People wonder about what you are pursuing.

You have to explain about the thread.

But it is hard for others to see.

While you hold it you can't get lost.

Tragedies happen; people get hurt

or die; and you suffer and get old.

Nothing you do can stop time's unfolding.

You don't ever let go of the thread.[3]

_____

_____

_____

_____

_____

_____

_____

---

3. William Stafford, *Ask Me: 100 Essential Poems* (Minneapolis, MN: Graywolf, 2014).

4. Consider the following benediction and how it might correspond
   to the idea of accompaniment and its components.

For a Leader

May you have the grace and wisdom
To act kindly, learning
To distinguish between what is
Personal and what is not.

May you be hospitable to criticism.
May you never put yourself at the center of things.
May you act not from arrogance but out of service.

May you work on yourself,
Building up and refining the ways of your mind.

May those who work for you know
You see and respect them.

May you learn to cultivate the art of presence
In order to engage with those who meet you.

When someone fails or disappoints you,
May the graciousness with which you engage
Be their stairway to renewal and refinement.

May you treasure the gifts of the mind
Through reading and creative thinking
So that you continue as a servant of the frontier

Where the new will draw its enrichment from the old,
And you never become functionary.

May you know the wisdom of deep listening,
The healing of wholesome words,
The encouragement of the appreciative gaze,
The decorum of held dignity,
The springtime edge of the bleak question.

May you have a mind that loves frontiers
So that you can evoke the bright fields
That lie beyond the view of the regular eye.

May you have good friends
To mirror your blind spots.

May leadership be for you
A true adventure of growth.[4]

_____

_____

_____

_____

_____

_____

4. John O'Donohue, *To Bless the Space between Us* (New York: Doubleday, 2008), 151–52.

ATTENTIVENESS

Patience

Patience and I have traveled hand in hand
   So many days that I have grown to trace
   The lines of sad, sweet beauty in her face,
And all its veilèd depths to understand.

Not beautiful is she to eyes profane;
   Silent and unrevealed her holy charms;
   But, like a mother's, her serene, strong arms
Uphold my footsteps on the path of pain.

I long to cry,— her soft voice whispers, "Nay!"
   I seek to fly, but she restrains my feet;
   In wisdom stern, yet in compassion sweet,
She guides my helpless wanderings, day by day.

O my Beloved, life's golden visions fade,
   And one by one life's phantom joys depart;
   They leave a sudden darkness in the heart,
And patience fills their empty place instead.[1]

—Edith Wharton

---

1. Edith Wharton, "Patience," in *Selected Poems of Edith Wharton*, ed. Irene Goldman-Price (New York: Simon and Schuster, 2019), 289.

Chapter Two
ATTENTIVENESS

OBSERVATIONS

*Ten times a day something happens to me like this—some strengthening throb
of amazement—some good sweet empathic ping and swell. This is the first,
the wildest and the wisest thing I know: that the soul exists and
is built entirely out of attentiveness.*

—Mary Oliver

Attentiveness cultivates belonging and mattering. Belonging is when we have a sense that we truly fit. Feeling like we belong nurtures a sense of community. When you belong, you know you have impact and influence; you feel that you are making a difference, especially that you are making a difference that actually contributes to bringing about the Kingdom of God in our midst. When we matter, we know that we are acknowledged, regarded, and seen. We have a sense of significance; we have a sense of purposeful inclusion. Attentiveness is also a matter of perspective, which means that, as a leader in the church, your perspective needs to be God's perspective, that whom God sees we should see as well.

Every year the Minneapolis Institute of Arts hosts "Art in Bloom," an exhibit that features over one hundred and fifty floral arrangements interpreting various pieces from the museum's permanent collection. The exhibit is a remarkable convergence of past and present art, interpretation then and now, reflecting how meaning is contextually determined and defined, and how perspective matters. A few years ago, one artist represented a Renoir painting. Evidently, Renoir once said to Matisse: "When I have arranged a bouquet for the purpose of painting it, I always turn it to the side I did not plan."[2]

Our initial approach to a leadership challenge is similar. We arrange the bouquet, setting out the parameters of the issue. We lay out the information so as to solve the problem. The information is constituted of background, palates, and co mponents like depth, color, and texture to create an integrated whole, a presentable piece, and something that is certainly beautiful in its attention, intentionality, and detail. We step back and admire how it all fits together. We feel satisfied with our efforts to collate and coordinate seemingly disparate data into a dazzling display of deliberation. We marvel at the mystery that we have managed to contain for a minutely determined analysis.

Yet, the arrangement we have constructed becomes all too quickly a finality rather than a possibility for leadership. When information is perceived as sufficient for a leadership model, when we are so taken with models and arrangements, then we expect others will share the same viewpoint. We become lost in the picture we want to create, that we have painted in our minds, instead of allowing ourselves to be grasped by a perspective that might surprise us—or even approaching the bouquet with the hope that it will.

Renoir reminds us that the portrait we have constructed may not be that which we should paint. What happens when you turn what you have learned to the side for which you did not plan? What will come into view when you look at the entirety of the bouquet through the perspective of

---

2. Alastair Sooke, *Henri Matisse: A Second Life* (London: Penguin Press, 2014).

one flower? What will you see when you shift the lens ever so slightly, like the infinitesimal turn of a kaleidoscope?

Imagine what this means for the leader. Could leadership be an expressed art? You are a painter. A sculptor. Leadership is indeed interpreting in real time; leadership offers a perspective about direction for a certain purpose, place, and people. Leadership embodies the space that seeks to speak into time, interprets the present, and imagines possibility for the future. That is art. That is leadership. Leadership as art recognizes that tried-and-true methods of what leadership has been cannot always hold the tests of time. Leadership assumes and then asserts a kind of fluidity, not from the perspective that things happen independent of the Spirit but from the experienced truth that the Spirit is still at work.

As Matisse wrote:

> Each picture, as I finish it, seems like the best thing I have ever done...and yet after a while I am not so sure. It is like taking a train to Marseille. One knows where one wants to go. Each painting completed is like a station—just so much nearer the goal. The time comes when the painter is apt to feel he has at last arrived. Then, if he is honest, he realizes one of two things—either that he has not arrived after all or that Marseille...is not where he wanted to go anyway, and he must push farther on.[3]

Renoir and Matisse remind us of that which is beyond ourselves, beyond ourselves as leaders, beyond ourselves when it comes to our theological constructs, creeds, and confessions. These artists' views might very well prevent—albeit with prudence—our mind's eye's own myopic manifestations.

Perhaps, to lead is to enter into the arena of the artist, the reality of the performer, even the preacher, as one who seeks expression in time but also as one who understands the vulnerability of interpretation. To lead is to be one who knows the joy of creation while simultaneously being fully aware

---

3. Matisse, Masterworks from the Baltimore Museum of Art, Minneapolis Institute of Arts, February 23 to May 18, 2014.

of the world's critique. To lead means to be one who searches for meaning in the moment while also sensing time's fleeting serendipity.

Profoundly incarnational and profoundly biblical, leadership is being who you are in the moment into which you have been called. It is communicating your truth that then has to be articulated in a particular moment. It is risking a permanent expression of truth when you realize how impermanent truth really is. Attentiveness is living the life of an artist and should be central to the life of a leader. In other words, attentiveness exists in the moment.

As such, inattentiveness is the manifestation of leadership that either has turned in on itself or is so rudderless that it cannot see beyond the most immediate, and usually acute, needs. Taking a brief pause to ponder this truth will likely yield several noted examples. When leadership turns in on itself, and while the symptoms might vary, more often than not the root cause is an unhealthy situation. This can be an undiagnosed condition, such as a leader's narcissism or even a leader in over their head, filling a position in which they do not belong or for which they lack the skillset. Of course, the determined condition could be anything ranging from sickness and disease, to mental illness, addiction, or personal strife. For the Christian leader, an ability to recognize and diagnose the reason for inattentiveness is, in part, a mandate from God. One cannot lead if one is not well, if one is unable to see beyond the tip of one's nose. In other words, an inability to be attentive signals a much more pressing concern than distraction. Inattentiveness can also be a symptom of lacking empathy, a dangerous condition for any leader.

This means that spiritual health is essential to embodying attentiveness as a leader in God's church. Spiritual health is embodied health. The spirit, as the very breath we breathe, cannot be separated from the mind or the body. Spiritual health resides in the integration of our entire being and our bodies. You cannot lead attentively if the rest of your body, mind, and soul are preoccupied or busy with other tasks. This assumes that attentiveness is a full-body affair. The way you sense the needs of others and how you respond to these experienced concerns is never only a matter of gathering of information, establishing matrices, or creating charts. Rather, attentiveness comes with believing in and embodying the soul of God. Attentiveness can be felt in the very bowels of your body, much like how Jesus responded to the poverties of the crowds around him. Jesus's compassion for them is expressed as feeling concern in his very guts. This is the kind of attentiveness demanded of a leader in the church. Attentiveness is not sympathy or thoughts or prayers. Attentiveness is the visceral, gut-wrenching reality of truly seeing those consistently overlooked, of regarding those perpetually minoritized, of seeing those who long ago gave up on the hope of being seen. A leader in God's church recognizes that God calls the whole of us, not just parts of us; the whole of another, and not just a utilitarian section. We cannot compartmentalize one or two aspects of ourselves or others and then hope that the other parts will take care of themselves. The incarnation assumes that the entirety of what makes us human—body, mind, and spirit—will be present and embodied in how we lead. With God in mind, we hold ourselves to a standard of grace and not to perfection.

But we try, and try desperately, to lead perfectly, ignoring our health as if no one will notice. But God sees us. God cares for us. And God is invested in the whole of us. Embodiment is all but impossible if attentiveness is neither integrated nor incorporated. Attentiveness toward another is virtually unattainable without attention to yourself. In our eschatological imaginations, we assume the question we will be asked is: Did you love your neighbor? However, rarely do we expect the question for the promise of eternal life to be: Did you love yourself?

Theological attentiveness requires an integrated self—a self that tends to the body, mind, and spirit because it is through the body, mind, and spirit that God communicates, that God reveals God's self, and through which we embody God's love in the world. Theological attentiveness demands attention to the body, the whole of the body in all of its senses so that we can truly embody the perspective of God.

THEOLOGICAL PREMISE

Leadership is not being in charge, it is about taking care of people in your charge.

—Simon Sinek

Attentiveness as a Christian leader is born out of the incarnation. The very sending of Jesus, the very act of God becoming human, was an act of attentiveness, of a deep recognition and realization of missed relationships and an absence of love. It is in God's very nature to notice the lost, the overlooked, the abandoned, the hurting, the lonely, and the grieving. It is also in God's very nature to acknowledge when faithfulness to God and to one another is present, or not present, in the lives of God's people.

The Christian leader is, in part, a true rhetorician. In ancient rhetoric, the rhetor is someone who senses the poignancy of the moment and is able to speak into it. This is what embodied leaders do and know how to do. Embodied leaders recognize that sensing the poignancy of the moment demands attentiveness. They see around them the pathos of a situation, of a community, or even of the world, and then they offer a word that names both the truth of the situation, truths into circumstances, and the divine hope known in the promise of God's gospel. By *gospel* we mean not only the benefits and promises of Jesus's life, death, resurrection, and ascension but also what the incarnation fundamentally expresses: the presence of God.

Isaiah knew the meaning of the gospel:

Go up on a high mountain,
>   messenger Zion!
Raise your voice and shout,
>   messenger Jerusalem!
Raise it; don't be afraid;
>   say to the cities of Judah,
>   "Here is your God!"
Here is the Lord God,
>   coming with strength
>   with a triumphant arm,
>   bringing his reward with him
>   and his payment before him.
Like a shepherd, God will tend the flock;
>   he will gather the lambs in his arms
>   and lift them onto his lap.
He will gently guide the nursing ewes. (Isa 40:9-11)

In the Septuagint (the Greek translation of the Old Testament, or the Hebrew Bible), "herald of good tidings" is the Greek word for "gospel." Thus, it can also be translated as "the one who brings good news" or as "the one who gospels." A leader in the church is this very herald and is attentive to the needs of God's people; such a leader first and foremost announces: "Your God is here."

This is who God is; God has been attentive to the needs of God's people since the very beginning of the relationship that God established with God's people. God saw Sarah's shame and gave her a son. God saw the abandonment of Hagar and blessed her. God saw the hardships of God's people, providing water from split rocks, light to walk in the darkness, and bread from heaven. God came to God's people in the voices of prophets. God regarded Elizabeth in her barrenness, Mary in her compromised state, the bent-over woman, the widow of Nain, and even Zacchaeus up in the sycamore tree. God has always embodied attentiveness. God hears the cries of God's people and responds. God listens. As Bonhoeffer writes:

> But [the one] who can no longer listen to [others] will soon no longer be listening to God either; he [or she] will be doing nothing but prattle in the presence of God, too. This is the beginning of the death of the spiritual life, and in the end, there is nothing left but spiritual chatter and clerical condescension arrayed in pious words. One who cannot listen long and patiently will presently be talking beside the point, and be never really speaking to others, albeit...not conscious of it. Anyone who thinks that his [or her] time is too valuable to spend keeping quiet will eventually have no time for God and [others], but only for himself [or herself] and for his [or her] own follies....Christians have forgotten that the ministry of listening has been committed to them by [God] who is the great listener and whose work they should share. We should listen with the ears of God that we may speak the Word of God.[4]

Attentiveness is fundamentally a commitment to and awareness of the moment, whether that moment is between individuals or amongst members of a community. As someone said: "Stop waiting for Friday, for summer, for someone to fall in love with you, for life. Happiness is achieved when you stop waiting for it and make the most of the moment you are in now."[5] Theological attentiveness is both a commitment to the moment and a conviction that God is present in that moment. Theological attentiveness is having the same eyes as God; the same perspective as God, able to see where there is indigence and brokenness; and the same hearing as God. Theological attentiveness is determining a response that truly meets that moment and fits that moment like a missing piece in a jigsaw puzzle. We are willing to turn the floral arrangement ever so slightly. Our God has embodied attentiveness from before the beginning. When leaders in the

---

4. Dietrich Bonhoeffer, *Life Together*, trans. John W. Doberstein (New York: Harper & Row, 1954), 98.

5. Author unknown.

church show this same kind of attentiveness, then we are indeed embodying a theological attentiveness that the world has never seen before.

THE PROMISE OF THE *PARACLETE*

One doesn't have to operate with great malice to do great harm. The absence of empathy and understanding are [sic] sufficient.

—Charles M. Blow

A principle component of the *paraclete* in John's Gospel is the promise that the Spirit has the ability and capacity to attend to the perceived needs of the disciples. This is the very charge inherent to the identity of the *paraclete*. Of course, the entirety of the Farewell Discourse has been Jesus's embodiment of this truth. The Farewell Discourse is Jesus at his pastoral best, recognizing the fear, hurt, and pain of his disciples, both from the betrayal and foreshadowed denial in their midst and Jesus's predictions about his departure. Into these emotions, Jesus speaks words of comfort, truth, and hope.

While the Farewell Discourse is a culmination of this attentiveness on Jesus's part, Jesus has embodied attentiveness throughout the course of his ministry. Neither the invalid man in John 5 nor the man born blind in John 9 asked for Jesus's healing. Instead, Jesus saw them. Jesus noticed them, tended to their immediate situations, and offered relationship with him. Jesus brought them into his community, a community that they had never had before, as sheep of his own fold. Jesus's whole ministry is about tending to attentiveness, noticing, regarding, and in that heightened awareness, acting. For example, when Jesus hears that the religious leaders have thrown out the formerly blind man, Jesus finds the man (John 9:35). As soon as we interpret these kinds of acts as expected or assumed, as soon as we suppose that attentiveness is "natural" or "no big deal" then it ceases to be attentiveness. Attentiveness is hard work. It demands a kind of intentionality to look outside of ourselves when it is our human nature to be tuned into ourselves.

The *paraclete* enters into the space that will be vacated with Jesus's crucifixion, resurrection, and then ascension. It is a space that Jesus has inhabited in a particular way, meeting the myriad of needs that have come his way. Jesus knows that the disciples cannot go on without this kind of attentiveness, in part because attentiveness is inherent to intimate relationship. As a result, Jesus promises to send "another *paraclete*," just as he has been that *paraclete* leader all along.

The attentiveness of the *paraclete* is born out in the detailed designations of the *paraclete*'s activity and as it is interspersed throughout the Farewell Discourse. In other words, the activities of the *paraclete* are responses to the specific needs of the disciples in that moment. When the *paraclete* is first introduced, the *paraclete* follows after Jesus's first announcement that he is leaving. Thomas cries, "'Lord, we don't know where you are going. How can we know the way?'" (John 14:5). Responsive to his disciples' troubled hearts, Jesus announces the promise of the *paraclete*: "I will ask the Father, and he will send another Companion, who will be with you forever. This Companion is the Spirit of Truth, whom the world can't receive because it neither sees him nor recognizes him. You know him, because he lives [abides] with you and will be with you. I won't leave you as orphans" (John 14:15-18a).

The next occurrence of the *paraclete* comes in the midst of words about hatred, stumbling, expulsion, and execution. In chapter 15, Jesus introduced the image of the vine and the branches, the last "I AM" statement with a predicate nominative (that is, an "I AM" that is then followed by a statement that defines the "I AM."). The metaphor communicates intimacy and dependency, which the disciples need to hear before Jesus's command to love one another and bear fruit. The world that the disciples are called to love is also the world of betrayers (e.g., Judas, see John 13:30) and deniers (e.g., Peter, see John 13:36-38). It is the same world in which they are commanded to bear fruit, to witness to the presence of God in Jesus (John 4:34-38; 20:21), and the same world that will outright hate them—as we read in John 15:19: "This is why the world hates you." In chapter 16, Jesus predicts the following circumstances for the disciples: "I have said these things to you so that you won't fall away. They will expel you from the synagogue. The time is coming when those who kill you will think that they are doing a service to God" (John 16:1-2). In the midst of the certainties of hatred and stumbling, being thrown out of the synagogue, and death, Jesus offers these words about the *paraclete,* "When the Companion comes, whom I will send from the Father—the Spirit of Truth who proceeds from the Father—he will testify about me. You will testify too, because you have been with me from the beginning" (John 15:26-27).

As the disciples are asked to bear fruit and to bring witness of Jesus to a world that will hate them, a world that will find ways to make them stumble and will throw them out of their communities, and may even kill them, Jesus reminds them that the *paraclete* goes before them, giving witness on Jesus's behalf. The command to testify can only happen alongside the promise of the testifying *paraclete.*

The final reference to the *paraclete* in the Farewell Discourse embodies attentiveness to the disciples' grief, and even their agony, about Jesus's departure: "In the same way, you have sorrow now; but I will see you again" (16:22; 16:5-7). Jesus promises once again that he will send the *paraclete* so the disciples will not be alone. The *paraclete* will do the work of calling out the sin of the world, convicting the unrighteousness of the world, and exposing the true judgment—that the ruler of this world will never have power over God. Jesus realizes that all of which he speaks is too much for the disciples to hear, and it is into this anguish that the Spirit enters: "However, when the Spirit of Truth comes, he will guide you in all truth. He won't speak on his own, but will say whatever he hears and will proclaim to you what is to come" (John 16:13).

Just as Jesus has embodied attentiveness in his ministry and leadership, the *paraclete*, as the "another" that is Jesus, is shown to do the same. In particular, the *paraclete* attends to the disciples' very specific emotions, feelings, and concerns. This theological attentiveness both enters the situation and offers hope that this attentiveness is not fleeting. Theological attentiveness is never just a momentary fix but is a promise of a future grounded in relationship.

THE SAMARITAN WOMAN AT THE WELL

*Leaders who do not listen will eventually be surrounded
by people who have nothing to say.*

—Andy Stanley

The person who best embodies *Key Two: Attentiveness*, the kind of attentiveness Jesus demonstrates in his ministry and in his leadership in the Fourth Gospel, is the woman at the well (John 4:1-42). In her story, we see the primary manifestations of attentiveness: listening and conversation; alertness; responsiveness to signs of opportunity; receptiveness; acknowledgment; and praise.

The woman at the well is a rather surprising witness to the presence of God in Jesus, especially since, in chapter 3, the expectation is that Nicodemus, with his qualifications and status, would be the ideal new believer. The contrasts between Nicodemus and the woman at the well are striking. Nicodemus is a Pharisee, a leader of the Jews who also has a name. The conversation between Jesus and Nicodemus takes place at night in Jerusalem, which is the religious center of Judaism. The woman at the well is a religious outsider, a woman who has no name and who meets

Jesus at noon at Jacob's well outside of Sychar, a town in Samaria that is a religiously marginalized site.

The setting (John 4:1-6) sets up Jesus's reason for being at the well: Jesus has been in Jerusalem for Passover and is now traveling back to Galilee. Although the text reads, "Jesus had to go through Samaria" (John 4:4), this is not geographically true. Geographically speaking, Jesus did not have to travel through Samaria because there were other travel routes between Judea and Galilee, particularly routes that would not have required a Jew to travel through Samaria and thereby come into contact with a Samaritan (someone who would be considered ritually unclean). Rather, it was necessary for Jesus to go through Samaria because of the mandate of John 3:16: "God so loved the world that he gave his only Son, so that everyone who believes in him won't perish but will have eternal life." Jesus must go to Samaria to show the disciples what "the world" really means, what the phrase "God so loved the world" really looks like in action.

The encounter between Jesus and the Samaritan woman takes place at Jacob's well, which is a betrothal scene in the Old Testament. Moses and Sipporah, Isaac and Rebekah, and Jacob and Rachael all met at Jacob's well. Thus, the location sets the stage for the conversation about the woman's husbands and the reason for her being by herself at the well. In the New Testament scene, the disciples have gone into the city to buy food, thereby leaving the Samaritan woman and Jesus alone at the well (John 4:8). By being alone together at the well, they were violating every political, social, and religious boundary.

The conversation between Jesus and the woman at the well unfolds in the following structure: The Setting (4:1-6); The Encounter (4:7-10); The Possibility (4:11-15); The Heart of the Matter (4:16-19); The Inquiry (4:20-24); The Revelation (4:25-26); The Invitations (4:27-30/4:31-38); and The Witness (4:39-42). Before moving through the conversation's content, it is important to note that it is a conversation—a conversation between two people who should not be talking to each other in the first place, and yet the conversation models a way of discourse for leadership in the church. As someone once said, "Discussions are always better than arguments, because an argument is to find out who is right, and a discussion is to find what is right."[6] The fact that there is a conversation at all communicates the importance of dialogue for faith and for leadership. The narrative space given to this dialogue demands that we pay attention not only to the *what* of the conversation (its content), but also the *how* of the conversation. It is in the *how* of this dialogue that we see a model of attentiveness. In the Gospel of John, and even in the whole New Testament, this is the longest conversation that Jesus has with any individual. There will be other lengthy conversations that take place with groups of people, but there is no other encounter that compares to this one between Jesus and the unnamed Samaritan woman at the well.

After establishing the setting for the conversation, the initial encounter happens when Jesus arrives at the well and asks the woman for a drink. The woman immediately points out that on many levels—political, social, religious—this conversation should not be happening: "Why do you, a Jewish man, ask for something to drink from me, a Samaritan woman?" (John 4:9). This beginning part of the conversation embodies what attentive listening looks like and sounds like. While it may seem that Jesus's answer is given in a kind of cryptic-code language, he has directly responded to the primary issue of her question: Jesus's identity. The Samaritan woman says that he is a "Jewish man," and Jesus replies, essentially, "no, I am God's gift to you" (John 4:10, paraphrased). He speaks directly to the main point of her inquiry, which also happens to be one of the main theological themes in the Gospel of John. The Samaritan woman is alert in her navigation of Jesus's answer, immediately picking up on Jesus's phrase "living water" (v. 10). Although she initially interprets Jesus's words

---

6. Author unknown.

literally, replying, "Sir, you don't have a bucket and the well is deep," she is open to hearing more about Jesus's proposal, asking, "Where would you get this living water?" (John 4:11). Jesus hears in her question her openness to what he has to offer, even an openness to who Jesus really is. Even though this initial part of the conversation remains on the surface level of knowledge and inquiry, it ends in possibility and receptivity. Already with her answer, "Sir, give me this water, so that I will never be thirsty and will never need to come here to draw water," the woman at the well has moved farther along in her conversation with Jesus than Nicodemus had (John 3:9; John 4:15). Although her understanding of what Jesus is extending her is still at a kind of literal level, she recognizes that Jesus has something she needs—he is the source of a neverending supply of fresh water, essential for her livelihood and the life of her community.

Into this openness to possibility, and because of her receptivity, Jesus then moves the conversation forward by asking her to call her husband. Because he is Jesus, he knows her; he is aware of her situation and realizes that this request goes to the very heart of the matter, the heart of her pain, her suffering, and her shame. Jesus does not ask her to get her husband because he wants to expose her, blame her, or rub salt in her wounds. Rather, Jesus says, "Go, get your husband, and come back here" (John 4:16) to get her to see his truth, that he is the Truth, just as he sees her truth. She then speaks her truth, saying, "I don't have a husband," and Jesus acknowledges that truth, a truth that was likely the reason she was at the well by herself in the heat of the day, although it was customary for women to fetch water in the cool of the morning or at dusk (John 4:17). She was likely alone at the well because no one wanted to be around her and have her sin rub off on them, the assumed reason for her marital bad luck. Having five husbands, of course, was not anything over which she had control. For her to have had five husbands would mean that her husbands either died or divorced her. If widowed, she would need to remarry if there were no male heir. If she was divorced it was likely because she had been unable to produce an heir. A woman in first-century Palestine would have had no agency in her marital status and no grounds for divorce. The man, on the other hand, could divorce his wife for whatever reason he deemed necessary, determined, or desired. Jesus knows her most excruciating truth—that she has been either widowed or divorced and has probably been discarded because she was barren. He also knows that she is now in a levirate marriage, where the brother of a deceased man is obligated by law to marry his brother's widow (Deuteronomy 25:5-10). Because of this exchange, she sees that Jesus is a prophet, as prophets in biblical times were first and foremost truth-tellers. The Old Testament prophets were only predictors of the future insofar as they were able to interpret the past and the present as a continuing trajectory. But, of course, Jesus is more than a prophet—he is the very presence of God.

Because of this budding recognition of Jesus's identity, the woman at the well then realizes that Jesus might have the answer to the most pressing theological issue that had separated the Samaritans and the Jews for centuries: where to worship God. After the Babylonian captivity, when the Jews and the Samaritans were allowed to return to Palestine, the Samaritans built their temple on Mount Gerizim and the Jews built their temple in Jerusalem. There was no possible way for them to worship in the same place because the Samaritans were considered unclean for having intermarried with foreigners. The Samaritan woman seizes this opportunity to engage Jesus in a substantive theological debate, and Jesus engages back. In doing so, Jesus intimates the real truth of his identity—the Word made flesh—by saying that the place to worship the Father is "neither on this mountain nor in Jerusalem" (John 4:21).

A careful and deliberate reading of this conversation up to this point should demonstrate what attentiveness looks like in action. Both the woman at the well and Jesus embody the kind of attentiveness essential for Christian leadership: being alert, receptive, open, and responsive. It is not a conversation centered around critique or criticism, on polemic or point-scoring, on hiding the facts or agendas, on competition or come-uppance, but grounded in a kind of deep mutual regard that mirrors the attentiveness of God. This profound reciprocity is embodied fully in the next phase of the conversation, The Revelation (John 4:24-25), where, in response to the woman's question about where to find God, Jesus reveals his true identity: that he is God, "I AM." While most translations read, "I am he," the pronoun "he" is not in the Greek text. Jesus simply says, "I AM," which was God's revelation of God's very self to Moses (Exodus 3:13-15). A review of the absolute "I AM" statements in the Gospel of John (the "I AM" statements that are not followed by a disclaimer or identifier) confirms that this is the first absolute "I AM" statement in the Gospel of John. In this mutual truth-telling moment, Jesus reveals his true identity, not to the disciples, not to the religious leaders, but to a nameless woman, a religious outsider, a social outcast. She tells her truth and Jesus tells his. Attentiveness, it seems, involves truth-telling reciprocity.

What follows in the rest of the story is an embodiment of reciprocal acknowledgment and praise. In response to Jesus's revelation, the woman embodies an essential feature of discipleship in the Fourth Gospel: witness. In John, witness or testimony is an expression of acknowledgment of identity and, in particular, of praise. To witness to Jesus is to do what John the Baptist had already done, which is to say, "Look!" (John 1:29, 36) when you recognize God in your midst. To witness to Jesus, to praise Jesus, is not when you have all of the answers ("He cannot be the Messiah, can he?") but is an invitation: "Come and see." Conversely, Jesus praises the woman's witness. When the disciples return from town, Jesus turns an invitation to lunch into an invitation to witness: "I am fed by doing the will of the one who sent me and by completing his work. Don't you have a saying, 'Four more months, and then it's time for the harvest'? Look, I tell you: open your eyes and notice that the fields are already ripe for the harvest" (John 4:34-35). In other words, "See what the woman just did, by going back to her townspeople and inviting them to abide with me? That is what being my disciple looks like. That's what witness looks like." Not only does Jesus acknowledge the woman for her attentiveness but Jesus also publicly praises her for embodying the results of her attentiveness.

The entire conversation, the interaction, is what theological attentiveness entails. The woman at the well embodies attentiveness by her active listening, her questions, her openness, and her courage. This is the kind of attentiveness that the church needs, an attentiveness that is not listening so as to respond but is listening so as to be challenged and changed.

FURTHER REFLECTION

Being heard is so close to being loved that for the average person they are almost indistinguishable.

—David Augsburger

1. Attentiveness as a Christian leader sets up a number of critical questions for how we go about the ministry of the church, particularly when we look at the story of the woman at the well. Reflect on the following questions:

Attentiveness notices who is present and who is absent. To use the metaphor of a table, particularly in the context of the aloneness of the woman at the well, we can ask: Who is sitting around the table? Who is missing? Were they not invited? If so, why weren't they invited? Did they feel like they did not belong? Who is hosting the table? Who determines the topic of conversation? Who gets to speak, and who is silenced? It does not matter how big the table is if someone still thinks they own it.

2. According to the story of the Samaritan woman at the well, attentiveness looks for and names where there is brokenness. Brokenness can be defined in a number of different ways: (1) violently separated into parts; (2) having undergone or been subjected to fracture; (3) not working properly; (4) not kept or honored; (5) disrupted by change; or (6) not complete or full.

In your ministry setting, where is there brokenness and why? How would you describe this brokenness—perhaps an incompatibility, a rift, dissolution, separation, division, or schism? How do you think, or do you know, how it happened? How are you being called to address the brokenness? Where do you see God at work to mend the brokenness?

_____

_____

_____

_____

_____

_____

_____

_____

_____

_____

_____

_____

3. On the other hand, attentiveness also notices connection. Connection might be viewed in the following ways: as a relationship in which a person, thing, or idea is linked or associated with something else; having something in common; a place where two or more things are united; having shared interests or efforts; or joining two or more things into one.

Where do you see connection in your ministry setting? Where do you realize relationship, interdependence, attachment, and bonding? Where has connection been lost? Why was connection lost? What will it take to restore connection? What might God be doing to restore connection that you, as *paraclete*, can name?

4. The opposite of attentiveness is a lack of empathy that can be summarized by the "prayer" below. Consider how and why this prayer is the opposite of attentiveness. For each line, map out the corollary if attentiveness is the operative principle.

A Narcissist's Prayer

That didn't happen.

And if it did, it wasn't that bad.

And if it was, that's not a big deal.

And if it is, that's not my fault.

And if it was, I didn't mean it.

And if I did

You deserved it.[7]

_____

7. Author unknown, http://narcissisticandemotionalabuse.co.uk.

5. Reflect on the quotation below. How does it speak to your understanding of attentiveness? These words acknowledge that attentiveness will bring to the surface realities of hardship and even
sin. Attentiveness is not just paying attention but is a willingness
to enter into those places of pain. Attentiveness is also a willingness to give witness to how, as leaders, we testify to the joys and
celebrations of those in our charge, especially those unable to
give voice to moments in which they have felt disregarded.

Do not be dismayed by the brokenness in the world. All things break.
All things can be mended. Not with time, as they say, but with intention.
So go. Love intentionally, extravagantly, unconditionally. The broken world
awaits in darkness for the light that is you.

—L. R. Knost

Chapter Three

AUTHENTICITY

Witness (John 20:15-18)

I carry the witness of Mary
in my body.
It is good news.
That I am alive is proclamation;
my presence announcing:
I have seen the Lord!
Every step I take
takes him further and further away
from the tomb.
Yes, I carry the witness of Mary
in my body.
And, dear woman,
you do, too. [1]

—Annie Langseth

---

1. Annie Langseth, 2020. Used with permission.

Chapter Three
AUTHENTICITY

OBSERVATIONS

When a toxic person can no longer control you, they will try to control how others see you. The misinformation will feel unfair, but stay above it, trusting that other people will eventually see the truth just like you did.

—Unknown

Why is authenticity so hard? Why is it one of those aspects of the human condition that we know is important to have, yet we have such a difficult time achieving? Authenticity offers a challenge like no other because you actually have to believe in yourself. And then, all too often, this belief in one's self is misconstrued as a kind of conceit or pride. Believing in yourself is antithetical to the gospel, critics claim. We believe first in God, trust first in God. This is true, of course. We cannot do what we do without absolute assurance of God's presence and promises. But we forget that God also trusts in us. God trusts those who have answered a call from God to lean fully into that vocation. Do we trust in ourselves as much as God does? Or do we go about our leadership in ways that betray a skepticism about God's intentions?

Authenticity is clearly not a biblical word, but its prevalence in contemporary parlance around leadership has a particular urgency when it comes to leadership in the church. The root definition of *authentic* is *real* or *factual,* with this subsidiary definition: "being true to one's own personality, spirit, or character."[2] In general, authenticity is a desired trait. No one wants to be labeled as fake or phony, spurious or disingenuous. Yet, we seem to have a high tolerance for those characteristics in leaders, or, at the very least, a kind of complacency around calling out false leadership. Authenticity is tricky. It is one of those "we know it when we see it" traits, but we cannot really offer a clear reason for why and when we recognize it. It is often simply a feeling, a certain sense of a person.

Authenticity is often absent because it requires vulnerability and exposure. Without pretensions, the truth of who you are can be seen—and many of us, especially leaders, do not want to be seen fully, lest our less-than-positive traits get unmasked. One of the most challenging aspects of authenticity is to accept that authenticity does not correspond to perfection. Authenticity is the consistency between identity and action, between character and praxis. Authenticity resides in the intersection at which point you perceive the Spirit leading to example and when you see example leading to a manifestation of the Spirit. This is, in part, why authenticity is so fragile. That convergence is the space of necessary contemplation and deliberate self-dialog, leading to this question: Does what I am about to do correspond with my true self? Is what is at stake for me guiding this decision? It is a precarious junction because it is the place where assumptions can take hold and take over, where we allow embedded expectations to drive our decisions. It is the place where we are tempted to sacrifice what we hold dear, what is deeply important to us, to placate others or smooth over conflict. All too soon we have left ourselves behind,

---

2. "Authentic," *Merriam-Webster Online Dictionary,* https://www.merriam-webster.com/dictionary/authentic, accessed February 14, 2020.

chasing after impossible perfection or the assumption that we can fully meet others' demands.

Of course, compromise is often necessary, even essential, for moving forward. The compromise, however, must be the result of intentional deliberation about why the compromise had to happen; what is lost and what is gained in the compromise; and even how you will navigate the compromise, given what you might have had to sacrifice. As Frank Ostaseski writes:

> What is authenticity? It is saying what is so when it is so. Showing up, doing what we say we will do, remembering our commitments, and honoring our agreements. Authenticity engages the will and points to what has heart and meaning, while simultaneously diminishing reactivity. It means taking personal responsibility for both the tasks at hand and the relationships we build as we perform those tasks. Acting authentically builds trust.[3]

As a result, there is a lot at stake when it comes to authenticity. Honest mistakes become personal missteps. Miscalculations become character flaws. That is, we trade authenticity for bargains that mask our true commitments, for deals that we can then justify later as essential moves in the game. Instead of admitting that we are imperfect beings, leaders often avoid such personal discomfort by hiding behind deference. We would rather buy into a kind of socially acceptable set of leadership traits than risk embodying characteristics that might lead to questioning our leadership. We would rather overcompensate, especially in those skills most valued, than be labeled a failure.

We all make mistakes. As a popular saying goes: "I've learned so much from my mistakes, I am thinking about making a few more of them." Or, in these words often attributed to Eleanor Roosevelt, "Learn from the mistakes of others. You can't live long enough to make them all yourself."

---

3. Frank Ostaseski, *The Five Intentions: Discovering What Death Can Teach Us about Living Fully* (New York: Flatiron Books, 2017), 128–29.

Indeed, mistakes are inevitable and we can undeniably learn from them. However, these quotations are less than helpful when mistakes are given a kind of permission to shortchange the self-reflective process. When mistakes become excuses. When mistakes are allowed to validate experimentation without vision and authorize innovation without responsibility. When mistakes are written off as appraised ideas and there is no attempt to engage in a critical self-analysis toward avenues of change. There needs to be a balance between a healthy sense of risk to try new things and make mistakes and considering where, how, and why the missteps happened and what has to change going forward. When this self-reflective process is truncated, stumblings turn into behavioral traits and are then needlessly, and sometimes harmfully, perpetuated.

Rather than fess up to these errors and blunders, we cast blame. Authenticity, therefore, demands apology. An authentic leader anticipates having to apologize but does not defer to apology as a way of escaping accountability. In other words, true authenticity requires an ability to take responsibility for one's actions and demands publicly acknowledging when faults have occurred. Accountability and responsibility are hallmarks of authentic leadership. As such, authenticity is visible in how we lead but perhaps even more so in how we negotiate those moments of lapsed judgment.

THEOLOGICAL PREMISE

Some of the best advice I've been given: don't take criticism from people you would never go to for advice.

—Morgan Freeman

Authenticity, from a theological and biblical perspective, therefore, calls for confession. If any public body can embody what confession looks like, it is the church. The church regularly engages in confession to remind itself of what it is but also to acknowledge when it has fallen short of what

God has called it to be. It is the church's vocation to embody confession, especially confession that articulates how it has not fully proclaimed the truth of the gospel and when it has not fully participated in bringing about the Kingdom of God.

Inauthenticity, therefore, is born out of fear—a fear of failure. A fear of being exposed as an imposter of sorts, as someone who does not belong in this position, as someone who accidently ended up with this appointment, that this turn of events must be some sort of fluke, a professional anomaly. A fear of making wrong decisions, even the fear that you made the wrong decision in the first place by accepting a call to this leadership position. As noted above, embodying authenticity in leadership is first and foremost trusting in God, especially trusting that God indeed called you and called the entirety of you. You might not believe in yourself, but it might make a difference if you trust that God believes in you. That is the hallmark of theological authenticity—a certainty that your authentic expressions of leadership are God-confirmed.

We take our cue from Paul and his narration of what happened to him on the road to Damascus. There is Luke's version as told in Acts chapters 8 and 9, and then there is Paul's testimony in Galatians 1:11-17. At stake for Paul is the very gospel itself—that God reconciled to God's self the entire world through the death and resurrection of Jesus Christ. Yet, what has surfaced in Galatia is a willingness to comply with criteria for belief that are outside of the promises of Christ. Paul then asserts that his call is not something he manufactured but was equivalent to the calling of the prophets. His was a call from God.

That is, authenticity for a leader in the church needs to have some sense of a call, some sense of an outside mandate, and some sense of God's belief in you. If we base our authenticity solely on our confidence in our abilities, in our own capacities, or in the admiration of others, then we have entirely failed to understand the promise of theological authenticity. We have bought into the belief that the only person, thing, or premise on which we can regularly count is our own self. Such constructions determine authenticity outside of the church but are antithetical to the truth of authenticity for the church. When it comes to authenticity in leadership in the church, the core principle has to be: Does this manifest, articulate, and reveal the event of Jesus Christ? This is the fundamental criterion for Paul. Or have we adopted or co-opted a kind of authenticity devoid of the experience of the risen Christ? The authentic leader in the church believes in this promise: "However, when the Spirit of Truth comes, he will guide you in all the truth. He won't speak on his own, but will say whatever he hears and he will proclaim to you what is to come" (John 16:13).

As Howard Thurman writes, "There is something in every one of you that waits and listens for the sound of the genuine in yourself. It is the only true guide you will ever have. And if you cannot hear it, you will all of your life spend your days on the ends of strings that somebody else pulls."[4] You will indeed be pulled in multiple directions. One of the challenges of public leadership is that if you are swayed to follow a path in which you do not believe or which does not represent your true self, then it will be observed and observable. You cannot hide inauthenticity. Authenticity, inherently, is known in embodiment. You cannot tell people you are authentic or make an argument for the ways in which you are authentic. You either are or you are not.

Embodying authenticity as a mark of integrity in leadership in the church is not going to be found in well-meaning advice or pithy sayings in scripture. Authenticity is an implicit trait of those called to lead God's people, whether in the Old Testament or in the New Testament. The theological premise for authenticity for leaders in the church is, once again, the incarnation. God entered into humanity as fully human, as flesh, and nothing short of the fullness of that truth will suffice if one is a leader in

---

4. Howard Thurman, "The Sound of the Genuine," baccalaureate address at Spelman College, May 4, 1980, https://www.uindy.edu/eip/files/reflection4.pdf.

God's church. We might like to say that we affirm this promise of God, that God knows completely and utterly what it means to be human, but we still do not want God to be aware of where we do not measure up in this whole being human thing. There is only so far we are willing to imagine God's patience with our own humanity. God's divinity often gets in the way, and then we have a tendency to expect divinity from ourselves. While we are partial to the idea of God being human, and even confess it on a weekly basis, it often makes us uncomfortable. It means that God knows us all too well. We might be able to hide our hearts from the people for whom and with whom we do ministry, but that is an impossibility when it comes to God. The satisfactions and hazards of authenticity come into full view.

It seems that there is more at stake when we fail in ministry. We have not only failed our congregations, the people in our particular ministry settings, but we have also failed God. It is hard enough to imagine those times when we have let down those who have counted on us, who trusted us; it is nearly impossible to imagine what it feels like to disappoint God.

Perhaps, however, this is essential for authentic leadership in the church: that what is distinctive about how we lead is that something is at stake for God. This is not an injunction to try to earn God's favor. Our actions and our behavior can never measure up to secure God's grace. At the same time, however, we do have an accountability to God's vision for the world and to expediting God's kingdom here on earth. To bring about the kingdom does indeed set out certain standards, not to be met, because that is God's business, but that by which our leadership should be judged. At the end of the day, we are beholden to a different "boss," if you will, and that obligation should provide some perceivable assessment of the authenticity of our leadership. If authenticity is to be true to one's spirit, as leaders in the church we are then called to be true to God's Spirit. We simultaneously discern the correspondence between our actions and our spirit and evaluate our actions as they match with the activity of God's Spirit. How we lead is an embodiment of the nature of God's Spirit.

Authenticity is an urgent matter for leaders in the church because we are the alleged holders of the truth—in all of its manifestations. We are the assumed keepers of the truth of the Bible and its authority. We are the supposed keepers of the truth that is Jesus Christ: "I am the way, the truth, and the life" (John 14:6). For good or for ill, we are recognized as the resident biblical scholars and the resident theologians. Authority is given to us to tend to sound biblical interpretation and to make sense of God's activity in the world. Finally, we are the professed keepers of the truth of God—that we have had the necessary training and needed experience to lead a congregation in discerning what God is up to and how it can be a part of God's mission.

As a result, when authenticity comes under scrutiny, so also does our capability to take care of this trifold truth. If we are not living in and acting out of our own truth, how then can we be keepers of God's truth? There will be a disconnect between our perceived authority and the kind of authority we give to God's truth, however that might be defined.

Authenticity within a theological framework, because it has to navigate the tension between human frailty and flourishing, demands a commitment to regular confession and forgiveness. From a theological perspective, accountability and responsibility command acts of confession. We acknowledge, publicly, where we have sinned and fallen short of the glory of God. We ask for forgiveness and spend time reflecting on the meaning of that forgiveness, on what it feels like to be forgiven, and on how we will change our actions going forward. Trusting in God's forgiveness, we are then able to accept that forgiveness from those whom we have wronged, even though that might not be immediate or even possible. At the same time, such awareness does not prevent us from confessing.

The opposite of confession is denial, and denial is the manifestation of inauthenticity. Inauthentic leaders deny culpability and defer accountability. Denial is the solution to avoiding the truth of compromise and the discomfort of exposure. Denial appears to be the best possible answer when you cannot face your inability to risk being seen. Denial, therefore, is a sign of the inauthentic leader. It is a symptom of distrust of the self, a deeply embedded insecurity.

THE PROMISE OF THE PARACLETE

When you let go of what no longer serves you,
you create space for what's meant to be.

—Unknown

You will never speak to anyone more than you speak to yourself
in your head, be kind to yourself.

—Unknown

Don't compare yourself with others. No one can play your role better than you.

—Unknown

One of the roles of the *paraclete* is to guide into all truth. "However, when the Spirit of Truth comes, he will guide you in all truth. He won't speak on his own, but will say whatever he hears and will proclaim to you what is to come" (John 16:13). Within the larger themes of John's Gospel, this intimates a connection to Jesus as the light of the world. The dominant meaning of the word *light* in the Gospel of John is to communicate a person's closeness with or relationship to Jesus. If someone is in the light, for example the woman at the well who meets Jesus at noon, then that person is seen to be in relationship with Jesus. On the other hand, if someone is in the dark, then that person's relationship with Jesus is questionable and subject to scrutiny. Thus, Judas's betrayal, where betrayal in

John means to abandon a relationship with Jesus, is cast as Judas going to the dark side: "He left immediately. And it was night" (John 13:30). Furthermore, light exposes. Light reveals. Try as you might, you cannot hide from the light. While Jesus does not come to judge or condemn the world, we bring judgment upon ourselves when we reject God's love revealed in the Word made flesh: "This is the basis for judgment: The light came into the world, and people loved darkness more than the light, for their actions are evil" (John 3:19).

A *paraclete* leader both stands under God's truth and speaks up about God's truth. We stand in the light, knowing that the light will also display and disclose. Either way, a Christian leader cannot escape the truth, the truth about one's self and the truth about God. Accountability to the truth is a characteristic of the Christian leader.

How does a Christian leader get at this truth? There are many truths about God, both named in scripture and held in the public sphere. Authenticity as a leader means that you can articulate your personal theological commitments because it is this truth, or a set of truths, that identifies and shapes your leadership. If you assent to truths that you deem are demanded or expected, whether by your denomination or another authority, even though that set of truths might be valid for that authority, they may not be your truth. Therefore, they will not, in the end, represent your authentic theological self. This is not about ascertaining *correct* theology. It is about discerning *your* theology. The entirety of scripture upholds that theology is not an objective science but the public testimony of one's experience of God. In fact, the whole of the New Testament is witness to the fact that what was thought about God is now a matter of reinterpretation because God is now up to something new in Jesus Christ. The basis of theological authenticity is to be able to claim and to interpret your own experiences of God. To interpret these theological experiences is a fundamental activity of authenticity. It is not enough to testify to an experience of God as special or unique; the next essential step is to engage in constructive theology born out of that experience. Leaders in the church must inquire of themselves: Who is God for you? What are the main characteristics of God to which you adhere? How does God primarily act in the world? Your answers to these questions should be the theological foundation on which you base your leadership.

A helpful exercise to access your core theological commitments is to ask yourself the following questions: What is your favorite Bible verse, passage, or book? Why is this your favorite? This verse, passage, story, or book is likely your embedded theology in a nutshell. It connects with you because it represents who God is for you and who you believe yourself to be in the eyes of God. This verse, passage, story, or book is likely what is at stake for you theologically and by which you should chart your leadership path. What is your theological truth that standing in the light of Christ, that the Spirit's guidance, reveals? Can you draw a line from this Bible verse, passage, or story to how you embody your leadership? Why or why not? Are the decisions you make, your leadership style, your set of priorities, and your mission or vision traceable to this Bible verse, passage, story, or book? Are you able to follow the thread from this Bible verse, passage, story, or book to how you embody the many spaces and places of your leadership role, how you interact with your staff, and how you engage the people in your ministry setting?

Theological authenticity is what distinguishes a Christian leader from other leaders. Theologically authentic leaders embody their theology in all that they do and say. This does not preclude disagreement or dissatisfaction. Not everyone will agree with, or even like, your theological commitments, but they are yours, and what will be noticed is the authenticity that makes them known. Like the *paraclete*, it is truth-speaking. "It is saying what is so when it is so."

MARTHA, THE SISTER OF MARY AND LAZARUS

*When someone spews something really hurtful don't pick it up and hold it and
rub it into your heart and snuggle with it and carry it around for a long time.
Don't even put energy into kicking into the curb. You gotta see it
and step OVER it or go AROUND it and keep on going.*

—Brené Brown

The character in the Gospel of John that best embodies *Key Three:
Authenticity* is Martha, the sister of Mary and Lazarus and a friend of
Jesus. We are not certain if the Mary and Martha of John are the same
Mary and Martha of Luke. Even if the stories of these women come from
the same source, John either knows a variation of the story or reworks
it for his own theological purposes, and their roles in each Gospel are
profoundly different. In John, Martha is a character that could easily be
overlooked, especially if our harmonizing ears equate her with the Martha
of Luke's Gospel.

The setting for Martha's interaction with Jesus is the sickness and then
death of her brother, Lazarus (John 11:1-44). The raising of Lazarus in the
Gospel of John is the last of the seven signs Jesus performs, and it results
in the religious authorities wanting to have Jesus arrested and put to death
(John 11:53). The sign is narrated in a different fashion than the other
signs in the Gospel (these signs are never called miracles in John's Gospel). For most of the other six signs, as Jesus performs each one, the sign
is followed by a dialogue or discussion about its meaning. Following this
is Jesus's discourse on, or interpretation of, the sign, which is important
because signs can be easily misunderstood. If signs point to something
beyond themselves, then the purpose of the signs in John is to direct our
attention to what the sign reveals about Jesus.

In the case of Jesus's raising of Lazarus, however, this pattern is re-
versed: the dialogue and the discourse about the sign take place before
the actual miracle because, as the last sign, it cannot be misinterpreted.

The raising of Lazarus is a foreshadowing of Jesus's own resurrection and, therefore, the promise of resurrection for all believers. At the same time, the promise of the raising of Lazarus, which is eternal life, is not just a future certainty but also a present reality.

Martha's tear-filled words embody the kind of authenticity that is essential for Christian leaders. First, she does not hide her grief or her distress; as we read in John: "Martha said to Jesus, 'Lord, if you had been here, my brother wouldn't have died'" (11:21). Martha's disappointment is even more poignant in Greek. A better translation of the sentiment behind her statement would be: "Lord, if you had been here—but you were not, my brother would not have died—but he did." She names boldly that Jesus has let her down, unabashed about how Jesus has failed her, and does not try to mask her lament. At the same time, she demonstrates that she has confidence in Jesus because she trusts him: "Even now I know that whatever you ask God, God will give you" (v. 22).

Following Jesus's promise, "Your brother will rise again" (John 11:23), Martha is not hesitant about offering up a statement of her belief: "I know that he will rise in the resurrection on the last day" (John 11:24). Her confession is not quite right, and Jesus corrects her: "I am the resurrection *and the life*" (John 11:25, emphasis added). Jesus needs her and everyone else to see that resurrection is not just a future promised life with God but is offered here and now through Jesus, the I AM. This eschatological inbreaking is the revelation in this exchange; otherwise, the meaning of the resurrection is relegated to that which happens to us after we die and the resurrection will have no meaning in our present. We then do not look for places and spaces of immediate resurrection in our midst. We might very well pass by a moment of new life right in front of us.

Martha does not let a fear of being wrong prevent her from uttering what she believes. We sense in her dialogue with Jesus both honesty and genuineness. Martha does not try to impress Jesus, nor is she looking for his favor, but her spirit voices what she knows to be true, especially when that truth is so very hard to admit. Even in a moment of pain and disappointment, Martha makes no attempt to hide behind more acceptable responses or to abscond to anticipated emotions. Instead, Martha shows us that it is in these moments of true vulnerability that authenticity is most needed.

Martha knows in what she believes and states that belief without reservation. As noted above, it would be easy to pass over a character like Martha, who only appears here in the entire narrative of the Fourth Gospel. Yet, this is no "usual" location or run-of-the-mill miracle. It is no accident that for this last sign John turns our gaze to Martha. At this most critical juncture, Martha's exchange with Jesus is the focus of an example for what authenticity looks like. The Gospels are replete with characters whom the evangelists hold up as models of discipleship, and more often than not, these characters are not those whom we would expect. Those in perceived leadership positions are not the ones who embody the kind of leadership to which Jesus seems to be pointing. In the Gospel of John, for example, it is neither Nicodemus, who is a Pharisee and leader of the Jews, nor one of the disciples who represent true leadership, but the unnoticed and unexpected characters like Martha.

Furthermore, Martha embodies what happens when a leader is trusted, when a leader is authentic. Martha might not trust the situation, for she has questions and concerns, and she is hurting and angry, but she trusts Jesus. She knows who Jesus is. She has a relationship with him. So she calls out the disconnect between the circumstance and who she knows Jesus to be; she expects Jesus to clarify this disconnection. She expects, even demands, that Jesus provide answers to what Jesus had promised. Of course, we do not know the back story or the details of their relationship. But the interchange in this last chapter narrating Jesus's public ministry intimates that they are close, that the relationship is such that we can presume reciprocity.

What occurs after the raising of Lazarus also indicates the close relationship between Jesus and Martha. Mary and Martha host a meal for Jesus in their home, the home they share with their brother Lazarus. The meal is not just an expression of gratitude to Jesus for raising their brother from the dead. Mary's washing of Jesus's feet is an intimate act, one that signals her deep love for Jesus. She loves Jesus abundantly, just as Jesus loved Lazarus abundantly and just as Jesus will then love his disciples abundantly by washing their feet (John 13:1-17).

In Martha, therefore, we witness a disciple who is both authentic and who recognizes the importance of authenticity in a leader. She speaks her own truth but also expects Jesus to embody his truth. While we are not privy to the details of how long they have known each other, how they met, or how often they saw each other, her expectations of Jesus convey that she was justified in what she said to Jesus and what she asked of Jesus. Martha's expectations convey that the way Jesus had been with her all these years had nurtured trust. She had no reason to doubt that she could say what she needed to say. Martha believed that what she knew about Jesus could be trusted even in that moment, a moment in which much was at stake. Therein lies the heart of authenticity.

FURTHER REFLECTION

Self-care means giving the world the best of you rather than what is left of you.

—Katie Reed

Thinking about how you react to and engage in authenticity, particularly as you see yourself as a leader of the church, is a necessary process that demands theological engagement. What follows is an opportunity for you to focus this intentional reflection around authenticity in embodied leadership. Therefore, consider the following questions, statements, and readings. As noted above, this is an important part of where and how this material might actually make a difference for your ministry and, in particular, how you see yourself as a leader of the church.

1. Determine your favorite Bible verse, passage, or book as a way to discover your core theological commitments that shape your leadership. What is at stake for you theologically? How does this biblical story, passage, or book help you define your theology in a nutshell?

2. Are you able to remember a time when you made a decision in your leadership based on your theological convictions, or a time when you had to defend your theological commitments in putting forward a decision? How did it feel? Was there any resistance?

3. Let us consider what Emily McDowell writes:

> "Finding yourself" is not really how it works. You aren't a ten-dollar bill in last winter's coat pocket. You are also not lost. Your true self is right there, buried under cultural conditioning, other people's opinions, and inaccurate conclusions you drew as a kid that became your beliefs about who you are. "Finding yourself" is actually returning to yourself. An unlearning, an excavation, a remembering who you were before the world got its hands on you.[5]

This is the hard work of this chapter, asking the questions: What is your true self? What is your authentic self? On what will you stake your theology? How will you lead intentionally from those core theological convictions?

_____

_____

_____

_____

_____

_____

_____

_____

_____

_____

_____

---

5.   Emily McDowell, https://emilymcdowell.com.

4. Reflect on this blessing for leaders by John O'Donohue. Where do you see the connections between the discussion of authenticity above and the language of the blessing? Do you think you might be able to embody these promises?

For One Who Holds Power

May the gift of leadership awaken in you as a vocation,
Keep you mindful of the providence that calls you to serve.

As high over the mountains the eagle spreads its wings,
May your perspective be larger than the view from the foothills.
When the way is flat and dull in times of gray endurance,
May your imagination continue to evoke horizons.

When thirst burns in times of drought,
May you be blessed to find the wells.

May you have the wisdom to read time clearly
And know when the seed of change will flourish.

In your heart may there be a sanctuary
For the stillness where clarity is born.

May your work be infused with passion and creativity
And have the wisdom to balance compassion and challenge.

May your soul find the graciousness
To rise above the fester of small mediocrities.
May your power never become a shell
Wherein your heart would silently atrophy.

May you welcome your own vulnerability

As the ground where healing and truth join.

May integrity of soul be your first ideal.

The source that will guide and bless your work.[6]

_____

6. John O'Donohue, *To Bless the Space between Us* (New York: Doubleday, 2008), 147–48.

5. Reflect on the following reading by Hildegard of Bingen and how
   you see it relating to the topic of authenticity.

O Ignis Spiritus

O fire of the comforting Spirit,
life of the life of all Creation,
you are holy in quickening all Kind.

You are holy in anointing
the dangerously stricken;
you are holy in wiping
the reeking wound.

O breath of holiness, O fire of love,
O sweet draught in the breast and flooding of the heart
in the good aroma of virtues.

O purest fountain, in whom it is seen
that God has summoned the gentiles
and sought out the lost.

O mail-coat of life and hope
of binding all the members of Ecclesia,
O sword-belt of honesty, save the blessed.

Guard all those who have been imprisoned by the Enemy,
and release the fettered
whom Divine Power wishes to save.

O most steadfast path which penetrates all things;
in the highest places, on the plains,

and in every abyss
you summon and unite all.

Through you the clouds stream, the upper air flies,
the stones have their temper,
the waters lead forth from their rills
and the earth exudes freshness.

You also always lead forth the comprehending
made joyful by the inspiration of wisdom.

Whence praise be to you
who are the sound of praise
and bliss of life,
hope and richest gift
giving the rewards of light.[7]

---

7. Hildegard of Bingen, "O Ignis Spiritus," https://allpoetry.com/O-Ignis-Spiritus.

Chapter Four

ABUNDANCE

God, of thy goodness, give me Thyself;

for Thou art enough for me,

and I can ask for nothing less

that can be full honor to Thee.

And if I ask anything that is less,

ever Shall I be in want,

for only in Thee have I all.[1]

—Julian of Norwich

---

1   Julian of Norwich, *Love's Trinity: A Companion to Julian of Norwich* (Collegeville, MN: Liturgical Press, 2009).

Chapter Four

God Alone Is Enough

Let nothing upset you,

let nothing startle you.

All things pass;

God does not change.

Patience wins

all it seeks.

Whoever has God

lacks nothing:

God alone is enough.[2]

—St Teresa Avila

---

2   St. Teresa Avila, https://www.poetseers.org/spiritual-and-devotional-poets/christian
/teresa-of-avila/prayers-and-works/.

Chapter Four
ABUNDANCE

OBSERVATIONS

The test of our progress is not whether we add more to the abundance of those who have much; it is whether we provide enough for those who have too little.

—Franklin D. Roosevelt

Stop the glorification of busy. Busy, in and of itself, is not a badge of honor. It is okay not to be busy. Repeat this with me: It is okay not to be busy.

—Joshua Becker

No leadership in the church can be leadership without a belief in and expectation of abundance. Why? Because most of the world operates out of a place of scarcity, from budgets that then drive decisions and determine the bottom line. The implicit belief is that more is better. Period. Or, if less is projected by statistics and collected data, by projections and analyses of trends, then practicality replaces hope.

Leadership in the church has to have at its core the belief in and imagination for the promise of abundance because the very heart of God is abundant grace. It is out of abundance that God does what God does and is who God is. The church's starting point matters. On what will we base who we are and what we do? Where will we begin? Beginnings shape capability and possibility. They set the tone for what is to come. Beginnings, starting points, are like first impressions, and it is much harder to correct a bad first impression than it is to put in the work to create a positive first one. Having a starting point of abundance changes everything. You expect to see it and cannot help but work toward it. A grace-upon-grace mentality never settles for a balanced budget but believes that a vision of abundance leads toward that for which it intends.

Leadership in the church always has in mind more than what seems potential or practical. Abundance is God's "operating principle," if you will; abundance is God's "mission statement." Yet, the dominant language of the church and its subsidiaries these days is one of decline. Obsessed with decreased attendance and the waning of denominational allegiance, we sit around looking at charts and graphs, hoping that the pendulum will swing if we just stare at it long enough. When flourishing, which is another word for abundance, is defined and determined by numbers, abundance will easily be overlooked. Abundance then ceases to be a theological category and is simply a mark of success. Yet, should not the church define what success means for the church rather than adopting an external definition of success? If we were to engage some serious analysis as to whether or not our plans for success were measurable against that which marked the gospel's success, there would likely be little alignment. We might question if this comparison of success is really fair when the church has changed so drastically since its beginnings. Yet, this is not a matter of comparison so as to retrieve a long-lost ideal, nor is it a back-to-basics mentality. Rather, the parallel is meant to expose the theological heart of the church. The church ceases to be church when it cannot remember its true calling—to witness to life in the midst of death, to testify to an empty tomb—neither of which is an acceptable indication of abundance.

The church is increasingly concerned about its demographics, that is, the average age of its membership. The longtime loyalty of older members has dissipated, either because of death or church conflict, sending congregations looking for followers who will agree with their theological commitments. The "nones" and millennials are the target audience, not unlike the strategic marketing of the entertainment world. We pander to the eighteen- to thirty-four-year-olds as if new can ever replace memory or vitality knows more than tradition. In all of these endeavors, the church has aligned itself with the rest of society, where the people who do not fit into the ideal demographic are pushed to the margins as irrelevant and are certainly not considered those on whom the church is willing to bank its future.

Abundance has also been replaced by innovation. Innovation is the answer to everything, from addressing the clergy shortage to programs that are certain to reboot your ministry, rejuvenate your congregation, and renew the church. However, these "shiny new objects" have a shelf life and are more often than not repackaged offerings from years past. Cast into the framework of innovation, the tried-and-often-true efforts of previous generations are suddenly the answers to all of our church woes. But innovation has a short-term memory.

Furthermore, innovation has also replaced the theological promise of new creation. Fundamentally, the promise of abundance lies in God as creator, our God who is able to create wonders out of nothing, who brings what is dead to life. When the church looks to innovation instead of to resurrection, it is no different than the church in Galatia. The Jewish missionaries who arrived at the Galatian congregation offered a kind of certainty for church membership. Circumcision, then, was the guarantee for being part of the body of Christ. However, the only certainty or guarantee for "church membership" is Christ's death and resurrection.

Were Paul here now, we might expect him to utter similar words to us as he did to the Galatians: "I'm amazed that you are so quickly deserting the one who called you by the grace of Christ to follow another gospel. It's not really another gospel, but certain people are confusing you and they want to change the gospel of Christ" (Gal 1:6-7). To paraphrase Paul, is the church seeking human approval or God's approval? Or is it trying to please people? If it is bent on pleasing people, in the end, the church is not a servant of Christ (Gal 1:10). *Galatianism* is alive and well in the church when it looks toward a humanmade solution to growing the church instead of trusting in God's determination—the only reason the church has survived this long in the first place.

Our human tendency is to assume that we need to work for the abundance granted to us rather than imagine how what we do is only possible because of the abundance we already have. Overworking in the church is an acceptable, even desirable leadership trait, as if our unceasing work could procure the abundance we so desperately seek. Admirable, even desirable, is the church leader who offers everything to the church. After all, the self-sacrifice of the church's leaders matches the sacrifice of Christ, as if that could ever be possible. Church leaders have convinced themselves that part of their job is to secure abundance. But in the words of Eugene Peterson, "If you don't take a Sabbath, something is wrong. You're doing too much, you're being too much in charge. You've got to quit, one day a week, and just watch what God is doing when you're not doing anything."[3] Abundance can once again be unnoticed when we have convinced ourselves that we, in the end, are its source.

When abundance is no longer understood as a theological category, it is then subject to the critique of practicality. The narrative goes something like this: "The church has to be practical, especially in these times

---

3. Joshua Lujan Loveless, "Eugene Peterson on Being a Real Pastor," *Relevant*, June 7, 2011, http://www.relevantmagazine.com/next/blog/6-main-slideshow/1262-eugene-peterson-on-being-a-real-pastor.

of uncertainty about its future. It's not in the church's best interest to engage in ministry that is not carefully calculated, particularly from a budget standpoint. These are not best practices." This is all the more true in times of crisis—ecclesial, financial, or a national or global crisis. Suddenly, abundance is now equated with frivolous behavior or irresponsibility, throwing caution out the window, pursuing reckless activities.

It is imperative in church leadership to reclaim abundance as a theological category. Leaders in the church must insist that there is a difference between practicality and responsibility; and yet, to what or to whom is our responsibility? This is the primary question. Clearly, the church has to maintain fiscal accountability and practice good stewardship of its resources. This has always been our calling, from the beginning of our creation. Abundance is not casting all cares to the wind with the hope that everything will work out in the end. Rather, the church is responsible to attend to the abundance already present from God's abundance. The gospel has never been practical. It challenged all expectations and upended all practicality. After all, that on which we could count, what in life is always certain, is now annulled—the empty tomb has silenced the cries of death. Death no longer has the last word. No one ever anticipated that the tomb would be empty. Even the first believers did not believe it. In fact, the initial response of the disciples to the good news of the empty tomb was: "That's total nonsense" (Luke 24:11). In this verse, the Greek word for *nonsense* is *lēros*, which can be translated as *garbage* or *crap*. Yet all too often, emptiness is viewed as dashed hopes, as more disappointment. Emptiness could not possibly indicate grace upon grace. But for the Christian faith, emptiness is indeed a sign of abundance. It is up to leaders in the church to tend this rather precarious space between responsibility and abundance so that abundance does not dissolve into a measured and meted-out ministry.

Furthermore, abundance is frequently synonymous with blessing. Articulating the difference between abundance and blessing is part of our calling as leaders in the church. Ironically, we want to hoard abundance. Our reaction to abundance is not necessarily to share or to be satisfied, but to protect it, even hoard it. Why? Out of fear? What is it that we fear? The human propensity for wanting more, for gathering up our mountains of things, is deep and wide. It perpetuates the divide between the rich and the poor. It determines who are the chosen ones and decides the identity of the cursed. It exposes our inherent insecurities—our self-doubts about our worthiness, our definitions of success, and even our views of grace itself. As if we believe that grace were merited and deserved or that grace were a reward and a validation.

While both abundance and blessing are most certainly theological categories, the latter has been coopted by "prosperity gospel" preachers and CEOs who have turned a blessing into a bonus, as something that has been earned, or as a proof of living the good life, whether that's living a life according to biblical mandates or just striving to be a moral person. In the framework of the prosperity gospel, your best life is somehow a manifestation of God's grace shining down on you for all to see. Whether it is a promotion with a raise, the closing on a dream house, or a sweet parking spot, *#blessed* is the explanation. And when blessing gets caught up in misconstrued abundance, the blessing is never enough. One is always looking for the next sign of being blessed, rarely happy with what one has.

According to the prosperity gospel, blessing, therefore, is connected with presumed good things and doing good deeds to warrant God's grace. In this framework, then, abundance is the observable result of blessing. That is, being blessed is much easier to see and to determine if there are quantifiers involved. The higher the numbers, the more blessing is certifiable. We want to be sure of it ourselves, and we also want others to come to the same conclusion. Blessing has a tendency to get caught up in concerns of misplaced security, and if abundance is present, then the more safeguarded we feel. As a result, a leader in the church has to name this insecurity, this all-too-human condition of worry, to which abundance is not the answer.

Leadership in the church is to lead from a place that assumes abundance, that pays attention to abundance, which gets embodied in gratefulness and graciousness. Consider the following quotation: "The root of joy is gratefulness....It is not joy that makes us grateful; it is gratitude that makes us joyful."[4] To live out of abundance is to know true joy, and joy is a manifestation of abundance. Embodied abundance is gratitude. But gratitude is not just sending a thank-you note from time to time. Gratitude, gratefulness, and graciousness arise from having been graced-upon-graced. They are acts of abundance in return because abundance begets abundance. This is the nature of abundance—it cannot *not* overflow: "We are cups, constantly and quietly being filled. The trick is knowing how to tip ourselves over and let the beautiful stuff out."[5] Leaders in the church are called both to embody gratitude and to practice gratitude. We are then called to encourage and empower believers in their lives to do the same.

THEOLOGICAL PREMISE

Sometimes I need only to stand where I am to be blessed.

—Mary Oliver

Wealth is the ability to fully experience life.

—Henry David Thoreau

---

4. David Steindl-Rast, *Words of Common Sense for Mind, Body, and Soul* (West Conshohocken, PA: Templeton, 2002).

5. Ray Bradbury, *Zen in the Art of Writing* (Joshua Odell Editions, 1996), 120.

We do not have to cast the net very wide to see how abundance is a sign of the inbreaking of the Kingdom of God, that God's reign has come, or that God's presence is in our midst. Abundance is a theological category, but it is not to be confused with blessing, as noted above. God is about blessing, conferring blessing is at the heart of God's nature, but also blessing is God's embodiment of abundance. Everything that God does is grounded in the nature of God's abundance and God's desire to create that abundance wherever God goes, and for whom anyone God meets.

If God's embodiment of abundance is blessing, then we see this played out in God's desire to be in relationship. For example, God had to establish a relationship with Abraham and Sarah because God could not keep God's abundance to God's self. The relationship that God establishes with Abraham and Sarah was blessing in and of itself, so that they were blessed to be a blessing. Abundance begets abundance.

The blessing bestowed upon Abraham was as innumerable as the stars in the heavens. Like Sarah, however, we have a hard time believing that such blessing, such abundance, could be possible. We laugh in the face of what we think is impossible, even for God. This is in our human nature. This is the human condition. As a result, it is up to leaders in the church to name this propensity, to name our human inclination to dismiss and even to decline God's blessing.

Repeatedly, God showers God's people with abundance, from manna in the wilderness to the blessing of the promised land. While the world only sees abundance in terms of an amount, leaders in the church know the truth about abundance that the rest of the world cannot see: that abundance is not a number but a sign of God's presence. When it comes to abundance, we can easily get sidetracked with numbers, quantifiable data, or measurements, when in fact, when it comes to God, the amount is really never the issue—as if we could compute abundance, and especially God's. The provision of manna in the wilderness wanderings, given day after day, was certainly an abundant source of food, but more so, it showed the Israelites that, indeed, their God was with them.

With abundance as a starting point, as that which is at the heart of who God is, we begin to see that the entirety of scripture gives witness to God's abundance. The New Testament writers see in Jesus God's abundance embodied once again. "God so loved the world" is a paraphrase of abundance; it is a restating of abundance, if you will. For Paul, Jesus is God's love for those outside of the covenant God had made with God's people. Jesus is a new covenant, not one to replace the old but one to show once again God's abundance. For the author of Luke-Acts, the gospel's reach is beyond measure: "Rather, you will receive power when the Holy Spirit has come upon you, and you will be my witnesses in Jerusalem, in all Judea and Samaria, and to the end of the earth" (Acts 1:8). For the Fourth Evangelist, God incarnated in Jesus is God's "grace upon grace" for the world (John 1:16). The Gospel of John's concluding verses refuse to cap God's abundance: "Jesus did many other things as well. If all of them were recorded, I imagine the world itself wouldn't have enough room for the scrolls that would be written" (John 21:25).

The ultimate sign of God's abundance is the resurrection of Jesus, and because of Jesus's resurrection, the resurrection of all believers. Abundance is a creation-out-of-nothing moment, a death-to-life moment. It is in these new creation moments that we have the greatest assuredness of God's presence because creation and resurrection are always God's doing. In other words, for God, abundance is never about counting numbers, comparing amounts, or claiming divine favor but is a recognition of and giving witness to God at work. Thus, to embody abundance is to work at being God's love for others.

It should be in the church where people observe this kind of embodied abundance. The church is called to point to these places in scripture where we see this abundance principle at work. For example, we read in Acts:

> A sense of awe came over everyone. God performed many wonders and signs through the apostles. All the believers were united and shared everything. They would sell pieces of property and possessions and distribute the proceeds to everyone who needed them. Every day, they met together in the temple and ate in their homes. They shared food with gladness and simplicity. They praised God and demonstrated God's goodness to everyone. The Lord added daily to the community those who were being saved. (Acts 2:43-47)

> The community of believers was one in heart and mind. None of them would say, "This is mine!" about any of their possessions, but held everything in common. The apostles continued to bear powerful witness to the resurrection of the Lord Jesus, and an abundance of grace was at work among them all. There were no needy persons among them. Those who owned properties or houses would sell them, bring the proceeds from the sales, and place them in the care and under the authority of the apostles. Then it was distributed to anyone who was in need. (Acts 4:32-35)

We might also describe this "abundance of grace" as hospitality, a synonym for showing love. Hospitality is not simply welcoming others or hosting a dinner party. Hospitality is a means by which we embody abundance. As such, leading with integrity in the church means following a command of hospitality. It means hosting spaces where abundance can be experienced, where mutual love is expressed. It means setting an institutional table where every place setting is a location of felt abundance.

When leaders in the church do not lead from this fundamental belief that our God is an abundant God, then we have eschewed much of the scripture's witness. If we do not embody God's abundance in our leadership, then our leadership will quickly devolve into a secular-blessing mentality that will most certainly contribute to the church's ever-diminishing numbers. The irony is palpable—the same church that is charged with giving witness to our God of abundance can only speak from its decline. Holding up abundance as essential for leadership in the church maintains the integrity of both scripture and of God.

THE PROMISE OF THE PARACLETE

Trust the wait. Embrace the uncertainty. Enjoy the beauty of becoming. When nothing is certain, anything is possible.

—Unknown

The *paraclete* itself is the presence and promise of abundance. Jesus has been among the disciples and in the world as God's grace upon grace. Jesus's ministry began with abundance—an abundance of wine at Cana—with every sign being an embodiment of abundance. Jesus's impending departure is the theological crisis of the Farewell Discourse, after which Jesus's going away, this grace upon grace, this presence of God, will end. The *paraclete* enters into that crisis, into that fear, to bring all that is needed so that even in Jesus's absence, the disciples will know that abundance remains. A *paraclete* leader will do the same. A *paraclete* leader will determine those places, and in those people, throughout the church and its institutions, where fear has taken over, where overwhelming wishes have clouded a vision of abundance, where weights and measures have replaced peace and hope.

Abundance is also expressed in new creation. The *paraclete* in John is also that which makes new birth possible again, anew, and from above (John 3:3). When the disciples lock themselves away after Jesus's crucifixion for fear of the same thing happening to them, Jesus appears among them to fulfill the promise he made in the Farewell Discourse: the sending of the Spirit. "Receive the Holy Spirit," Jesus says, after having breathed on them the Holy Spirit (John 20:22). Most of our translations, however, render the Greek verb incorrectly as *to breathe on*. The verb is not to *breathe on* them but *to breathe into* them the Holy Spirit. The verb in Greek, *emphusaō*, is the same verb used in the Septuagint (the Greek translation of the Old Testament) in Genesis 2:7: "[T]he Lᴏʀᴅ God formed the human from the topsoil of the fertile land and blew life's breath into his nostrils. The human came to life." It is also the same verb used in Ezekiel 37:9: "He said to me, 'Prophesy to the breath; prophesy, human one! Say to the breath, The Lᴏʀᴅ God proclaims: Come from the four winds, breath! Breathe into these dead bodies and let them live.'" For the disciples, this is a new birth—again, anew, and from above.

A *paraclete* leader will look for ways to give witness to God's creation and re-creation as a sign of abundance. We remind people that, in Christ, we are a new creation and that new creation is everything (Gal 6:15). A *paraclete* leader points to where God's abundance might be leading.

MARY WHO ANOINTS JESUS

Do the kinds of things that come from the heart. When you do, you won't be dissatisfied, you won't be envious, you won't be longing for someone else's things. On the contrary, you'll be overwhelmed by what comes back.

—Morrie Schwartz

In the Fourth Gospel, the character that embodies *Key Four: Abundance* outside of Jesus is Mary, the sister of Martha and Lazarus (John 12:1-8). We first meet Mary in chapter 11, but her role is more in the background as Martha's interaction with Jesus takes center stage. The opening scene of chapter 12 takes place in the house of Mary and Martha, to which they have invited Jesus after Jesus has raised Lazarus from the dead. Lazarus, the once dead man, is also there, reclining on Jesus. The setting itself brings to mind themes of abundance in that the once dead Lazarus, who had been in the tomb four days, has been resurrected and is now sitting at the dinner table with Jesus—talking and eating and drinking. Abundance is embodied in the resurrected body of Lazarus. The presence of Lazarus at the table is the "and the life" of "I AM the resurrection *and the life*" (John 11:24, emphasis added). Lazarus resting against Jesus is what "I came so that they could have life—indeed, so that they could live life to the fullest" looks like (John 10:10).

As abundance begets abundance, what follows next at this dinner party is Mary's embodiment of the abundance Jesus has already shown her in raising her brother from the dead. We cannot reduce Mary's washing of Jesus's feet to a mere sign of gratitude because in the very next chapter Jesus will carry out the very same act for his disciples. Jesus is not thanking his disciples preemptively for keeping his commandments. He is loving them abundantly so that they can then love abundantly, so that they can see to it that John 3:16, "God so loved the world that he gave his only Son, so that everyone who believes in him won't perish but will have eternal life," comes true. The abundance of love Mary shows Jesus is emphasized in the details of the anointing. Mary uses a pound of costly perfume, which we later find out was worth three hundred denarii, almost a year's wages. A pound is an inordinate amount of perfume, even too much, and our modern-day perfume is not nearly as fragrant as the nard with which Mary anointed Jesus's feet. The perfume is made of pure nard, meaning that it is not spliced with another element that would water down its potency. We are told that the house was filled with the perfume's fragrance, seeping into every nook and cranny. Like the wedding at Cana, the details communicate the abundance and, also like the wedding at Cana, the abundance is demonstrative of grace upon grace. The events in chapters 11 through 13, especially when they are read and heard together, underscore that abundance begets abundance.

What difference does Mary's act of abundance make, here and now? In Bethany, Jesus finds himself in a transitional time, place, and space, much like the wedding at Cana. Immediately after Mary anoints Jesus, he then enters the city of Jerusalem and walks into the last week of his life. He then says goodbye to his followers and prays for himself, for his disciples, and for believers yet to be (chapter 17). Mary's extravagant love for Jesus makes it possible for Jesus to show extravagant love in what follows—washing the feet of his disciples, handing himself over to be arrested in the garden, his trial, carrying his own cross, dying, rising, and ascending. Mary loves Jesus into his future as the fulfillment of "God so loved the world."

In other words, Jesus needed Mary's love as much as she needed to show Jesus how much she loved him. Jesus cannot do what he needs to do, has to do, or even wants to do, without being loved into his future. This mutual abundance is at the heart of Jesus's ministry, at the heart of Jesus as a leader. Jesus cannot show abundant love for his disciples without experiencing Mary's abundant love. There is a reciprocity here, a mutual need, between leader and those led that blurs the hierarchical lines we like to have drawn firmly and definitively. Jesus does not reject Mary's act of love or respond with, "Oh, Mary. That's not necessary." He does not spurn her expressions or feign a kind of mustered independence. Rather, Jesus accepts and receives Mary's love because he is in a place of great need.

We also know people who object to this kind of abundance, this kind of mutual love, who find it unnecessary or even a little over-the-top. There are those in our midst who will oppose an ethic of abundance, who will dismiss such abundance as wasteful, as certainly impractical, and definitely not helpful when it comes to the bottom line. There will be those among whom we lead and with whom we lead who think people are better off fending for themselves; that real strength means relying on individual fortitude rather than accepting "help" from others; that real power comes from trusting in your own autonomy and self-made success, rather than from dependence on others' hospitality. There are those who believe that faith and belief are best done on your own and not in community—after all, self-reliance is always safer than engaging in a group project. And yes, even in the church, there will be people who think that hospitality is the same as handouts or simply acts of kindness, or that pulling yourself up by your bootstraps is the ultimate act to guarantee God's blessing. Some in the church believe that abundance will somehow lead to unhealthy dependence and that real leadership should stand the hard ground of calculated risks, not extravagant gambles.

Lest we question these ecclesial propensities, Judas shows up in the middle of this act of extravagant love and embodies objection to abundance. Judas reminds us of these abundance resisters, of these people who either dismiss this kind of love or insist that only the weak would look for such prodding. Judas reminds us of these persons who, somewhere along the line, decided that the only future is the one they themselves determine. Judas reminds us of these persons who, for reasons we will never know, never experienced Mary's kind of love or have never believed that they were worthy of God's blessing. These abundance objectifiers are plentiful in parishes, even among those who have historically been generous in their offerings. Judas's defiance in the middle of Mary's abundance prompts us to wonder where we have opposed abundance and how that opposition has entrenched us in a scarcity mode far too long.

Jesus was loved into his future, first by his mother and now, here, by his friend. Jesus took Mary's love with him into Jerusalem. He acted out her love when he washed the feet of his disciples, especially when he washed the feet of Judas, who was about to betray him, and the feet of Peter, who would deny him. Jesus felt Mary's love, her gentle touch, once again when he was beaten. Jesus held on to Mary's love, desperately, when he hung on that cross. Jesus remembered Mary's love and then, once again, his mother's love when he looked into his mother's eyes one last time and said: "It is completed" (John 19:30). Then, Jesus took all of that love into the tomb, all of that love that would then love him into his future as the resurrection and the life. Are you, as a leader in God's church, willing to be loved in such a way so that you might embody that abundance in your leadership? That is the question that Mary asks us to consider.

Belief in and insistence on abundance is indeed risky business. Rejection is sure to follow when we hold onto abundance as a key to leading with integrity in the church. Abundance is vulnerable. Abundance intimates dependence. Abundance, in the end, cannot have a strategic plan because then it would not be abundance. Vulnerability and dependency are not character traits often valued in leaders in this day and age. Leading from the starting place of abundance anticipates awkwardness with many people and flat-out dismissal, even from those within the circle of the faithful.

FURTHER REFLECTION

*When life feels overwhelming don't be fooled into thinking that more action
is needed to create order and peace. Get quiet and go inside.
You'll find everything you need right there.*

—Unknown

1. In reflecting on the quotation above, do you have everything you
   need inside? What is missing? On what or on whom outside of
   you do you trust more than on whom God has called you to be?
   Why are you unable to recognize abundance? Are you resisting
   acts of abundance from others? If so, why? Of what are you fearful? Or what are you unwilling to discover about yourself?

2. Watch the following video from the perspective of abundance. An abundance perspective does indeed change everything for how we do church and talk about the purpose of the church. The video is "Easter Is Coming," by WorkingPreacher, posted April 1, 2010: https://www.youtube.com/watch?v=0c2inXKD6PI.

3. Who has loved you into your future? Who has, in part, made it possible for you to see yourself as a leader, and without whom you would have stayed where you were instead of being loved into that future? When have you loved someone into their future, even a future that is uncertain, even a future that will mean suffering? When have you embodied abundance, and how might you practice that on a daily basis in your leadership? How will you remind yourself to start from the place of abundance?

_____

_____

_____

_____

_____

_____

_____

_____

_____

_____

_____

_____

_____

_____

4. In *Lectio Divina* style, engage Psalm 23 from the perspective of the above discussion. The four steps of *Lectio Divina* are: *lectio* (read the psalm and then notice what words, images, or phrases capture your attention); meditation (meditate on or ponder the psalm, especially how the Holy Spirit helps you make connections between the psalm and the focus of this chapter); *oratio* (respond to the psalm and your reflections by praying, by engaging in a conversation with God); contemplation (sit in silence and stillness and allow the Spirit to work).

Psalm 23

The LORD is my shepherd.

    I lack nothing.

He let me rest in grassy meadows;

    he leads me to restful waters;

    he keeps me alive.

He guides me in proper paths

    for the sake of his good name.

Even when I walk through the darkest valley,

    I fear no danger because you are with me.

Your rod and your staff—

    they protect me.

You set a table for me

    right in front of my enemies.

You bathe my head in oil;

    my cup is so full it spills over!

Yes, goodness and faithful love

    will pursue me all the days of my life,

    and I will live in the Lord's house

    as long as I live.

Chapter Four

5. Reflect on the following poem. Does the poem help you make any additional connections between abundance and leadership?

Abundance

It's impossible to be lonely
when you're zesting an orange.
Scrape the soft rind once
and the whole room
fills with fruit.
Look around: you have
more than enough.
Always have.
You just didn't notice
until now.[6]

_____

6. Amy Schmidt, "Abundance," Poets Respond, January 20, 2019, https://www.rattle .com/respond/, accessed February 15, 2020.

ADVOCACY

The Magdalene's Blessing

You hardly imagined
standing here,
everything you ever loved
suddenly returned to you,
looking you in the eye
and calling your name.
And now
you do not know
how to abide this ache
in the center
of your chest,
where a door
slams shut
and swings open
at the same time,
turning on the hinge
of your aching
and hopeful heart.
I tell you,
this is not a banishment
from the garden.
This is an invitation,
a choice,
a threshold,
a gate.
This is your life
calling to you

from a place
you could never
have dreamed,
but now that you
have glimpsed its edge,
you cannot imagine
choosing any other way.
So let the tears come
as anointing,
as consecration,
and then
let them go.
Let this blessing
gather itself around you.
Let it give you
what you will need
for this journey.
You will not remember
the words—
they do not matter.
All you need to remember
is how it sounded
when you stood
in the place of death
and heard the living
call your name.[1]

—Jan Richardson

---

1. "The Magdalene's Blessing" © Jan Richardson from *Circle of Grace: A Book of Blessings for the Seasons*. Orlando, FL: Wanton Gospeller Press. Used by permission. janrichardson.com.

Chapter Five
ADVOCACY

OBSERVATIONS

*When a flower doesn't bloom, you fix the environment
in which it grows, not the flower.*

—Alexander Den Heijer

The primary translation for *paraclete* in most English Bibles is *advocate*. Of the different renditions of *paraclete*—comforter, aider, intercessor—*advocate* is the translation of choice, even when the activity of the *paraclete* in the moment is not best described as an advocate. Yet, this is indeed a primary action of the *paraclete*. Jesus sends "another advocate" because his leadership, as was his ministry, is one of advocacy. To embody Jesus as leader is to embody advocacy. Advocacy formally defined is the act or process of supporting a cause or a proposal. Advocacy can mean "speaking in favor of," "recommending," "arguing for a cause," "supporting or defending," and "pleading on behalf of others." Etymologically, in middle English *advocacie* means *intercession*; *advocassie* in Anglo-French means *pleading*, and in Medieval Latin, *advocatia* means *patronage*.[2] *Advocate* is,

2. "Advocacy," *Merriam-Webster Online Dictionary*, https://www.merriam-webster.com/dictionary/advocacy, accessed May 15, 2020.

of course, a legal term, meaning one who publicly defends another. For the Gospel of John, the principal act of advocacy is testimony or giving witness to God's presence in Jesus.

As noted before, Jesus introduces the *paraclete* when he speaks of his departure. Just as Jesus himself has witnessed to God as the "I AM" in the world, and as Jesus himself has stood up for and spoken up on behalf of his disciples, so also will the *paraclete*. The *paraclete*'s role as advocate is the overarching activity of the *paraclete* in the Gospel of John. When the *paraclete* is first introduced in the Farewell Discourse, it is clear that the *paraclete* will be the one to testify to the three fundamental truths of Jesus: Jesus's origin, Jesus's relationship with God, and Jesus's identity (John 1:1). Advocacy, then, is the fifth key to leading with integrity in the church. Advocacy grounded in a theological foundation has three expressions according to the *paraclete* in John's Gospel: advocacy for the self, advocacy for the other, and advocacy for the truth.

Advocacy is one of the most pressing challenges of leaders in the church today. Advocacy, by definition, is a vulnerable and public act that exposes your commitments. Once you stand up for something or someone, or even for yourself, you cannot take that action back. It is out there, and you are left only to navigate the consequences, whether for good or for ill. As a result, advocacy is one of the least practiced of Jesus's leadership identities.

Advocacy's absence is likely due to the assumption that it necessitates "taking sides." Once a leader, and particularly a leader in the church, is viewed as siding with certain people or issues, then the pastor is too political and cannot be a pastor to everybody. Standing up for a person or for an opinion does not automatically require rejection of the other person or the opposite stance. An inevitable refutation of the other is not always the case, but our human brokenness tells a different story. It is in our human nature to suppose that a vote for one side is a vote against the other side. It is also in our human nature to want our side to win, and to think that our side is the right side. And in the church, people want the pastor in their corner. Advocacy dances around these unspoken wishes, around these propensities of human sin that go unnamed. As such, in the church, any presumption of choosing a side is feared as a risk of alienating half of, or at least pockets of, the congregation. When the church already operates out of fear of losing more members, advocacy seems even more dangerous.

A misplaced and misconstrued definition of advocacy, however, has contributed to the church's loss of voice in the public sphere. Rather than rock the proverbial boat or risk being termed irrelevant, the church has stayed its course. The church cannot suddenly purport a prophetic voice when most of its preaching and teaching has held the invisible line down the middle of the road. Advocacy, however, is not taking sides but is an embodiment of integrity. While it may be true that a particular opinion is championed, at the very least you have acted with integrity. Advocacy demands honesty and uprightness. It calls for resolution and genuineness. Otherwise, it is little more than pandering or placation.

Leaders who are unclear about whom or what they are supporting will seem to lack confidence at best and appear untrustworthy at worst. Perhaps the most potent foe of advocacy is complacency. Complacency has led the church down some rather evil roads because it has been unwilling to speak out against all kinds of sin, including but certainly not limited to racism, sexism, heteronormativity, xenophobia, anti-Semitism, patriarchy, and white privilege. Fearful of losing members, or more likely, afraid of its diminishing power, the church finds itself in positions that are complicit with propositions antithetical to the gospel. The church has maintained its own forms of privilege, banking on members and donors to keep it going, accepting money from those with deep pockets and definite opinions, but have a shallow sense of the obligations of the gospel. The church and its subsidiaries have not had to face complicity in the privileges of the dominant society—white, male, middle-class, cisgender, and able-bodied identity. The church says it is about the behavior of the Beatitudes, but such behavior must include the kind of advocacy willing to call out injustice—not just hunger for righteousness.

Church leaders who do not have advocacy as a key to their ministry appear, well, wishy-washy. What is at stake for you? On what are you grounding your commitment to the gospel? Without determination and character, without a clear sense of strength or commitment, leadership becomes ineffectual, even banal. Knowing for what you stand embodies both advocacy and excellence—and it takes a great amount of courage to insist on both.

Another way to think of advocacy is allyship. An ally is defined as a member of a privileged group who works to enable opportunity, access, and equality for members of a nonprivileged group. Allies use their privilege and advantages to bring about change. Allies speak for those who cannot speak for themselves, all the while working to create spaces and places where silenced voices can be heard. Church leaders, and the church itself, have enjoyed centuries of privilege. Even with the critiques of authority and hierarchy over the last fifty years, the church is still afforded an ontological authority. That is, the church has authority simply because it is the church. Its authority is premised on its very being as church. But the landscape of religion in the last decades has exposed that this ontological authority is skating on thin ice or, more accurately, that the ice has cracked. The church can no longer assume its authority but has to substantiate it. Any kind of demonstration of authority in this day and age must be backed up with an evident sense of ownership and identity. There is a difference between a voice from the margins and a voice that has been pushed out to the margins because it no longer has anything to say. For the church's voice to get a hearing in the public sphere in today's society, it has to figure out something to say, something that will actually get heard. We should consider the antonyms of *advocacy* and ask: Does the church and its leaders want to be perceived this way, as baffling, foiling, frustrating, interfering, opposing, sabotaging, thwarting, deserting, disappointing, belittling, and letting others down? Perhaps the truth is that the church has more often embodied the opposites of advocacy and, in doing so, has failed the gospel. Allyship is a helpful and important value of advocacy, especially if advocacy is lodged too deeply in legal metaphors. Advocacy is not about winning a game, or about obtaining a favorable verdict in the courtroom, but about a lifelong commitment to solidarity with God's justice and with God's righteousness.

Rather than bemoan the continued marginalization of the church as our world becomes increasingly secular, it is time for leaders in the church to reclaim their identities as public theologians, advocating for the gospel's causes even in the face of certain rejection and dismissal. Church leaders are advocates when they stand up for what they believe in, thereby embodying integrity. They stand by those who are struggling to stand up for themselves; church leaders as advocates stand up for the Truth—with a capital "T." The gospel truth is not sound doctrine or confessional allegiance. When the truth of the gospel is dogma, advocacy quickly descends into partisanship. The Truth of the church is the person and presence of Jesus Christ, "I am the way, the truth, and the life" (John 14:6). To advocate for the Truth is not to ask, "What is truth?" (John 18:38) but to testify to *who* is the Truth. Most importantly, it is to witness to the presence of the Truth among us. Perhaps advocacy would be a higher priority in the church were we to imagine the Truth in our very midst.

THEOLOGICAL PREMISE

But I am not ashamed. I know the one in whom I've placed my trust.
I am convinced that God is powerful enough to protect
what he has placed in my trust until that day.

—2 Timothy 1:12

Throughout scripture, advocacy is vital in leadership roles. In Deuteronomy 9 Moses intercedes on behalf of the Israelites by reminding God of who God is and what God promises. This is a key component of advocacy, remembering for what you stand and for what you are "fighting," sometimes going up against significant power. It seems almost ridiculous that Moses thought he could advocate for God's people and get God to change God's mind. But Moses reminds God of God's promises. Advocacy does not always have to be adversarial. It can be a moment of compassion—to remind someone, or something, of true intentions. For example, it can be reminding a church council of the church's mission and purpose or reminding board members of the institution's mission and purpose, of why they are there in the first place.

The prophets themselves were advocates—advocates for God's character. They embodied the very voice of God and the heart of God, speaking the words of the Lord and from the Lord. As Cornel West says: "Prophetic beings have as their special aim to shatter deliberate ignorance and willful blindness to the sufferings of others, and to expose the clever forms of evasion and escape we devise in order to hide and conceal injustice…"[3] Advocacy's embodiment is admission. Advocacy's dismissal comes from denial.

In Jesus's first public act in Luke's Gospel, the sermon he gives in Nazareth, Jesus advocates for the poor and the oppressed: "The Spirit of the Lord is upon me, because the Lord has anointed me. He has sent me

---

3. Cornel West, *Democracy Matters: Winning the Fight Against Imperialism* (New York: Penguin, 2004), 114.

to preach good news to the poor, to proclaim release to the prisoners and recovery of sight to the blind, to liberate the oppressed, and to proclaim the year of the Lord's favor" (Luke 4:18-19).

In quoting Isaiah 61:1 here, Jesus makes it clear that his ministry is a continuation of the kind of advocacy God has always shown for the poor, the captive, and the oppressed. Jesus is certain on whom his ministry will be focused, and it is a clear stance of advocacy for the marginalized. At the same time, direct statements of beliefs cause the most opposition. Advocacy becomes adversarial not because you wanted or intended to be but because the people called out are forced to face their own principles. They have to decide whose side they are on, for what they stand, and for whom they would advocate. Such introspection is not always met with open arms or open hearts. People may feel shame and blame, not because that was your objective but because they have to come to terms with their own inabilities to advocate for themselves or for others, past or present. Advocacy is a mirror moment. When you witness embodied advocacy, you cannot help but question your own advocacy: where you have succeeded in advocacy and where you have failed in standing up for yourself, others, and the gospel's Truth.

Advocacy's mirror moment is often too much truth for people or institutions to bear, and as a result, the origin of the discomfort is seen as a threat. The informant, therefore, has to be "taken out." We see this all the time in our churches and especially in our political systems. The source of the dis-ease, the source that forced us to take a long and hard look at ourselves, is then maligned in some way: either someone's character or loyalty is questioned or it is decided that the source must be eliminated altogether. In the case of Jesus's sermon in Nazareth, eradicating the source is the chosen option; thus, the audiene is filled with rage and attempts to throw Jesus off of a cliff, just outside of town (Luke 4:28-29).

Paul, as both a prophet and an apostle, consistently embodies the role of the advocate and, in his case, as an advocate for the gospel of God, the gospel of Jesus Christ. His unwielding advocacy for the decisive event of Jesus Christ as having changed everything in Paul's life, especially challenging his understanding of God, can be traced throughout all of his letters. Whether you like Paul or not, his unswerving message, that the gospel of Jesus Christ is new creation for everything and everyone, is what advocacy looks like. The cause, that is, on what you stake your theology, is the litmus test for your leadership, and thus, it is clearly known to all. In other words, there is a correlation between and an integration of one's core principles and one's theology. Paul embodies theology in process, especially when that theology must be reworked because of an experience of God that calls forth obedience.

Advocacy, by its very definition, must be embodied. That for which you advocate is acted out in all that you say and all that you do. That which claims to be advocacy but which is not embodied is mere opinion. If you can keep it to yourself, it is not advocacy. If you act it out for the sake of an audience, it is not integrity.

THE PROMISE OF THE PARACLETE

There comes a time when one must take a position that is neither safe nor politic nor popular, but he must take it because his conscience tells him it is right.

—Dr. Martin Luther King Jr.

As noted in the discussion above, most English translations of the New Testament will render *paraclete* as *advocate*. This critical role of the Spirit first embodies what Jesus's ministry has done and then also reiterates the essential theme in John's Gospel of bearing witness. John the Baptist is not the baptizer but the witness, testifying to the light (John 1:6-8). Witnessing is the primary activity of discipleship in the Gospel of

John because, fundamentally, Jesus gives witness to God's presence. As the Word made flesh, Jesus embodies the presence of God among us.

Advocacy's role in leadership is introduced when it is the most necessary and in highly acute situations. The advocate shows up in the midst of the most difficult words Jesus has to say about what is to come, both for himself and for the disciples. This is the heart of what advocacy is all about. Advocacy shows up when it is most needed. Advocacy is embodied just when you would wish you could walk away. The advocate leader, according both to the *paraclete* and to Jesus, shows up and speaks out when you would rather remain hidden in the margins where silence is assumed and accepted.

Advocacy, when it is just the right time for it, should feel like the last thing you want to do. Advocacy asks for a public profession of self on the other's behalf, and when it comes to leadership in the church, advocacy asks for the Truth, for what the gospel is all about. As Jesus says in John's Gospel: "'I have spoken these things to you while I am with you. The Companion, the Holy Spirit, whom the Father will send in my name, will teach you everything and will remind you of everything I told you'" (14:25-26). Advocacy, embodied by the Holy Spirit, is sometimes reminders—in the case of the disciples, a reminder of all that Jesus has said to them—and how much more true this is for leaders in the church. Advocacy requires persistence and prompts us to answer to who we are, what matters to us, and why we do what we do. It is so easy to forget this center and to forget the Truth, especially in the face of ideas, models, and terminology that vie for our tired attention.

The advocate comes when the disciples are at their most helpless, wondering how to press on in the face of what is to come, how to hold it all together when their community, in the betrayal of Judas and the denial of Peter, is falling apart. This should be a signal for when, as a leader in the church, advocacy is most necessary, when you sense that people are ready to give up or give in and that they do not have much left. We see the signals when people are tired, tired of "fighting the good fight" and tired of apologizing for both the demise of the church and the detrimental actions of the church. People are tired of faith as sheer work that all too rarely seems to bring joy. Like the *paraclete*, the church leader as advocate then comes alongside, advocating for what makes all of our works, all of our efforts, worth it. The advocate stands up for the cause once again, because it is likely that the advocate is the only one who can.

MARY MAGDALENE

Someone, somewhere, is depending on you to do what God has called you to do.

—Unknown

In the Fourth Gospel, Mary Magdalene is the primary character who embodies *Key Five: Advocacy* as it had already been embodied by Jesus and the *paraclete* (John 20:11-18). The resurrected Jesus's appearance to Mary in the garden is the first of four resurrection appearances in the Gospel of John. After Jesus's encounter with Mary, he reveals himself to the disciples in the locked room (John 20:19-23), then again a week later to Thomas (John 20:24-31), and finally to Peter and the disciples on the shores of the Sea of Galilee (John 21:1-19).

The encounter with Mary is extraordinary on a number of levels. From a narratological perspective, Mary's individual meeting with Jesus mirrors Jesus's encounter with the Samaritan woman at the well. These two stories function as an *inclusio*, bracketing the Gospel with two examples of women who embody key components of discipleship and leadership, and especially embodying witness.

It should not be overlooked that the first resurrection appearance is to a woman. Given how much discussion there remains around women's leadership roles in the church, this simple truth—that Mary Magdalene is the first preacher of the resurrection—should silence any arguments against women's ordination, women as preachers, and women as leaders. The injunction of embodiment in the church is, as it has been presented in previous chapters, a theological demand of the incarnation. The Word became flesh, not *anthropos*, man. God's commitment to the entirety of the human experience, by definition, cannot preclude gender.

The appearance to Mary Magdalene takes place in a garden because that is the location of Jesus's tomb. Jesus's arrest, crucifixion, burial, and resurrection all occur in a garden, which is why, of course, Mary supposes Jesus to be the gardener. The setting is an important theological backdrop for Mary's embodiment of advocacy as the fifth key aspect of leadership in the church. The garden calls to mind the first biblical garden, the garden of Eden, from the first chapters of Genesis and the creation stories. John's Gospel opens with the exact first words of Genesis: "In the beginning." As a result, Mary's embodiment of the *paraclete's* role as advocate takes on greater theological weight than it would if this story were situated in a different setting. Mary's role as advocate in this place, at this moment, is as advocate for the entirety of God's creative and redeeming love for the whole world. Her embodiment of advocacy is for the sake of John 3:16— she is the advocate for the world God loves, the world that God created, the world with which God seeks to reconcile and to be in relationship once again.

In the initial exchange between Jesus and Mary Magdalene, Mary does not recognize Jesus at first. It is only when Jesus calls her by name that she realizes his identity. Mary's recognition of Jesus is first a response to hearing her name being uttered. She is, in that moment, and always has been, one of Jesus's sheep. The good shepherd knows his sheep by name, and they follow him because they know his voice (John 10:1-5). By hearing his voice and recognizing Jesus, Mary first embodies true discipleship, advocating for all of Jesus's disciples that who Jesus is, the good shepherd, is really true. She experiences it herself and it is to this truth that her response first gives witness. By calling Jesus *Rabbouni*, she initially acknowledges Jesus as her teacher, as her guide. It is an important affirmation of Jesus's leadership as well. She calls him *teacher* before she calls him *Lord*. She gives witness to this primary role of Jesus's ministry, this essential aspect of Jesus's leadership, before any other designation. In how Jesus lived, in how he accompanied his disciples, in how he engaged those whom he met, and in how he went about his ministry, it seems that what was observable on the front end was his embodiment as teacher.

Of course, by responding *Rabbouni* to Jesus calling her name, Mary then also recognizes and embodies her own identity as one of Jesus's disciples. There are many other titles by which Mary could have replied. Instead, *Rabbouni* is the title that embodies her own truth. In this brief exchange, Mary advocates for herself with the embodied response *Rabbouni*. She recognizes her own identity in that moment and gives voice to that identity.

Jesus then announces to Mary the good news of the resurrection. However, in the Gospel of John, the resurrection is the penultimate act of salvation. In Jesus's command, "Go to my brothers and sisters and tell them, 'I'm going up to my Father and your Father, to my God and your God'" (John 20:17), the promise in 14:2 is coming true: "My Father's house has room to spare. If that weren't the case, would I have told you that I'm going to prepare a place for you?" While the resurrection is indeed also promised, especially as Lazarus was raised from the dead, the ultimate salvation is the abiding place that Jesus is preparing for his believers. In other words, salvation in the Gospel of John is fundamentally a relationship with Jesus. As Mary realizes her own identity, Jesus then charges her with the salvific claim of the entire Gospel of John—Jesus is returning to the father, just as he had promised, and it is Mary who will announce this news.

Mary's announcement is an embodiment of all three aspects of advocacy: advocacy for the self, advocacy for the other, and advocacy for the truth. "I have seen the Lord" is first advocacy for herself. By shifting her perspective from the first person plural, "They have taken the Lord from the tomb, and *we* don't know where they've put him" (20:2, emphasis added), to the first person singular, she makes the promise her own. She stands up for her own experience and for her own interpretation of her encounter with Jesus. With this testimony and her first-person announcement, she faces the risk of disbelief and rejection. It is a courageous and bold move, one that shows us what embodying advocacy can look like.

Mary's exclamation, "I've seen the Lord!" also embodies advocacy for the other—the other, in this case, being both Jesus and his lordship. She advocates for Jesus's identity as Lord, to which John the Baptist first gave witness (John 1:23), taking a risk in advocating for who Jesus is. This is especially true when we remember that the Roman Empire executed Jesus. It is a remarkable act of advocacy to admit out loud that Jesus is your Lord and not the Roman Emperor, especially when the Jewish religious authorities have already said, "We have no king except the emperor" (John 19:15). It is even more remarkable to do so in the shadow of the cross and in the loneliness of an empty tomb. Mary chances not only personal rejection but also religious expulsion and death. Jesus had told the disciples that they will be put out of the synagogue for believing in him (John 12:42; 16:2), and the parents of the man born blind had the same fear (9:22). In fact, the religious authorities cast out the man born blind for seeming to be a follower of, or believer in, Jesus (9:34). Witness to Jesus's lordship—his origin and his identity—hazards great personal consequences. Now, after Jesus's crucifixion, to stand up for Jesus as Lord is not only to risk excommunication but could also result in death.

In the end, Mary Magdalene advocates for the Truth. Saying "I've seen the Lord!" (John 20:18) is a witness to "I am the resurrection and the life" (John 11:25) and a testifying to "I am the way, the truth, and the life" (John 14:6), to the truth of "I AM." In her witness, "I've seen the Lord!" is the embodiment of all testimony that took the chance to say, "Look!" (John 1:29), "Come and see" (John 1:39), "I was blind but now I see" (John 9:25), and "Sir, we want to see Jesus" (John 12:21). Mary advocates for the Truth while the other disciples have abandoned Jesus, hiding out behind locked doors. She speaks the truth to power, power that could crush her, whether that power be ecclesial systems or structures, practices or policies, worn-out doctrine or broken institutions. Mary continues to speak truth to power when we lift up her witness in our own naming of systemic sexism and misogyny, both in the church and in our culture. Mary Magdalene is what advocacy looks like embodied.

FURTHER REFLECTION

*Like a wildflower she spent her days, allowing herself to grow, not many knew
of her struggle, but eventually all; knew of her light.*

—Nikki Rowe

1. Can you identify one or two advocates in your life? If so, reach
   out to them and thank them. Determine if you might need their
   help yet again.

2. When and for whom have you filled the role of being an advocate? Or when and why have you been afraid to speak up?

_____

_____

_____

_____

_____

_____

_____

_____

_____

_____

_____

_____

_____

_____

_____

_____

_____

3. Reflect on the following reading as it connects to the issue of advocacy:

What do boundaries feel like?

It's not my job to fix others.

It's ok if others get angry.

It's ok if others say no.

It's not my job to take responsibility for others.

I don't have to anticipate the needs of others.

It's my job to make me happy.

Nobody has to agree with me.

I have a right to my own feelings.

I am enough.[4]

_____

4. Fariha Newaz, "Boundary Basics," July 26, 2018, https://urbanwellnesscounseling .com/boundary-basics/.

4. The following is a well-known and often-cited quotation by Martin Niemoller, a German Lutheran pastor who, along with others like Dietrich Boenhoffer, founded the Confessional Church in resistance to Nazi Germany, especially in resistance to Nazism's appropriation of the Protestant Church. How might you paraphrase this poem for your own time and place?

First they came for the Communists

And I did not speak out

Because I was not a Communist

Then they came for the Socialists

And I did not speak out

Because I was not a Socialist

Then they came for the trade unionists

And I did not speak out

Because I was not a trade unionist

Then they came for the Jews

And I did not speak out

Because I was not a Jew

Then they came for me

And there was no one left

To speak out for me[5]

---

5. Martin Niemoller, https://encyclopedia.ushmm.org/content/en/article/martin-niemoeller-first-they-came-for-the-socialists.

Chapter Five

5. Consider this poem as a measure of "success" as a leader:

If I Can Stop One Heart from Breaking

If I can stop one heart from breaking,

I shall not live in vain;

If I can ease one life the aching,

Or cool one pain,

Or help one fainting robin

Unto his nest again,

I shall not live in vain.[6]

---

6. Emily Dickinson, "If I Can Stop One Heart fom Breaking," *Hope Is the Thing with Feathers: The Complete Poems of Emily Dickinson* (Layton, UT: Gibbs Smith, 2019).

EPILOGUE

Epilogue

The body of God is soft.

She delights in her tummy rolls.

She takes pride in the strength of her thighs.

She rejoices in every curve.

She hides none of her body in shame. Every inch is beloved.

Your body is a site of the Divine.

In and through your body, you-enfleshed, we all come to know God.

Your body is blessed.

May you nourish it:

with love

with acceptance

with pride

with pleasure.

When you, when your flesh, is targeted with destructive lies, may you
hear the voice of God whispering to it tenderly,

"you are perfect as you are. you are beautiful. you are beloved. those who
speak violence are afraid to love themselves. be brave. love you. love
the glory of your form. there is no one right way to have a body."

If you love God, open yourself to the hard but healing work of loving
your body. You will find God there. Love one another's bodies. Love
all bodies. We cannot know God without bodies.

Thanks be for the flesh that reveals beauty, truth, and love.[1]

---

1. Enfleshed, accessed June 8, 2020, https://enfleshed.com/pages/miscellaneous-prayers.

EPILOGUE

ECCLESIAL IMPLICATIONS

In the end she became more than she expected. She became the journey, and like all journeys, she did not end, she just simply changed directions and kept going.

—R. M. Drake

Accompaniment, attentiveness, authenticity, abundance, and advocacy: the *paraclete* as a metaphor for leadership in the church embodies them all, as did Jesus himself. Jesus did not set out a leadership plan or a list of best practices for how to head a church. Instead, Jesus embodied who he was. *Embody* suggests that at the very least, we can strive to do the same.

There might be some pushback against this image for church leadership. After all, we are not the Messiah, the Son of God, or the Word of God. We cannot lead like Jesus did. But then, we will have missed the hope of this book. Jesus leads from who God is. We lead from who we are. This notion of leadership should be something for which we endeavor, or at least, something that inspires how we lead. And, who are we? Well, first and foremost, we are theologians. We believe that God has a stake in the church. It matters to God how we lead. Perhaps it might even be true that

God hopes we might lead as Jesus did. What if that were something we imagined as leaders in the church? That God really cares about how we embody Jesus's leadership? That it might matter to God that we model our ministry on how God's very self was embodied in Jesus's body and can be embodied in our bodies?

Truly, there are others in scripture who embody a Jesus model of how to lead. You may have additional biblical characters in mind who can serve as models for your leadership in the church. Here, however, are five women who, in the end, walked beside Jesus during his ministry and who help us see aspects of Jesus's own leadership embodied in others. In these five women, we see the very heart of the *paraclete* embodied, the very leadership of Jesus himself.

Perhaps, after reading this book, you are wondering if this is the metaphor for you, this idea of the *paraclete*. If it is not, what will yours be? What you choose, however, has to be what you live and how you lead. On what you decide to premise your leadership, if you are a leader in the church, demands a biblical and theological imagination. What will be the biblical image, the theological promise, that sets your leadership apart, both because of who you are and because you are a leader in the church? The essential key to leading with integrity in the church is simple: that how you lead flows out of what you believe about God. That who you believe God to be actually shapes how you lead. It is this integration that truly sets apart leaders in the church from leaders of other institutions. How the church leads is not necessarily ontologically superior to any other way to lead, but there should be a distinctiveness when one is charged with leading a *church*. God has chosen to reveal God's self through the work of the church. As such, it is our responsibility to tend to questions that should be asked of the church: What is church? What is the community of the faithful? What is the work of the church? What does it mean, and what does it look like, to live as a community in Christ? What is God up to in the church? Correspondingly, we should ask of ourselves, how does our leadership "answer" such questions. You are the church's representatives. Your leadership, therefore, communicates what church is, has been, and will be.

THEOLOGICAL IMPLICATIONS

Theology must always begin and always find renewal, not with words found in texts, but with the experience of actual human bodies.

—Luke Timothy Johnson

Most streams of Christianity hold that Jesus was fully human and fully divine, but we have a hard time living out the presumptions of this belief, especially when it comes to leading that which is charged with tending this belief—the church. When we separate Jesus's divinity from his humanity, we underestimate the potential and the offense of the incarnation in our teaching, preaching, and leadership. The incarnation, embodiment, has implications for how we think about God, the nature of vulnerability, self-image, disability, pastoral leadership, human dignity, community, and the hope of resurrected life. The very premises of Christianity are at stake in how we lead. Any religion that has incarnation at its center has to be interested in bodies. This should shape how we think and how we lead theologically. As Luke Timothy Johnson writes: "The task of theology is the discernment of God's self-disclosure in the world through the medium of the body."[2] Any religion that has a crucifixion at its center must be interested in bodies. This should shape how we view suffering bodies, abused bodies, and exploited bodies. Any religion that has sacraments at its center has to be interested in bodies because the sacraments are publicly embodied theology. The sacraments are the re-embodying of God's embodied Word; they are recontextualized embodiments of Jesus's life and

---

2. Luke Timothy Johnson, *The Revelatory Body: Theology as Inductive Art* (Grand Rapids: Eerdmans, 2015), 1.

presence and, as such, are significant acts of our leadership. Any religion that has an indwelling divine Spirit at its center has to be interested in bodies. This should shape how we anticipate seeing the Spirit at work in our world, and especially how we expect to see this Spirt at work in the bodies all around us. Any religion that has resurrection at its center must be interested in bodies. This should shape how we look for salvation in our world today. It should direct our attention to those bodies who testify to God's salvific activity. Finally, any religion that has community as its center must be interested in bodies. This should shape how the church's leaders, therefore, build and form community; it means that bodies are at the center of the church community; and it means that bodies are the object of the church's attention, both as loved by God and as those embodying the love of God.

A leader in the church lives in the intersection of God's word and world, striving to communicate to, within, alongside, and for the sake of those who need to hear God's love for the world and desire to see themselves as a part of that world. Leaders in the church are charged with giving biblical imagination to that which shapes the church and all of its subsidiaries. Church leaders embody how scripture helps us make sense of our lives. As such, making sense of how we lead finds its heart in scripture. Aware of the multiple complexities of contextualities out of which scripture speaks and into which it can bring a word of hope, the church leader looks to scripture, not to validate a certain kind of leadership but to trust in the Bible's testimony of where its writers were able to differentiate between God's leadership and the leadership of the world. It is our calling to help map that integration between the God we know in scripture, the God we have constructed, and the God we experience in our day-to-day lives.

So much of our lives, and the lives of the people with whom we do ministry, are lived in disconnection. Who we are at work is not the same as who we are at home. Who we are with family is not the same as who we are with friends. Who we are at church is not the same as who we are in our everyday lives. Compartmentalizing is our way of coping with an inability to integrate. The church perpetuates this decoupling when it keeps the issues of our days out of the pulpit or the worship service, when it does not help people interpret the world through the lens of scripture or through the eyes of God, and when its leaders are unable to ground their leadership in biblical and theological principles.

At stake in church leadership today is the relevancy of the Bible, of faith, and of the church. Where there is a lack of integrity, expect disinterest and disengagement to follow. Where there is a lack of embodiment, expect a dismissal of bodies as locations of experiences of God. We are then left with a disembodied religion, something to be studied rather than something to be felt. Something to understand rather than something that is revealed. Something that can be contained rather than something that invites us into accompaniment of, and with, the Divine. We are left with a disembodied God when God gave up everything to become flesh.

LEADERSHIP IMPLICATIONS

If they don't give you a seat at the table, bring a folding chair.

—Shirley Chisholm

Once we have embodiment at the core of what we do, we cannot help but see it everywhere. We cannot help but figure out how to do it. We stop shrinking to try and fit into expectations and models that have nothing to do with the church. We stop trying to mold ourselves into forms that do not have a stake in the incarnation. We stop avoiding embodiment—because God knows, we avoid it. We are fully aware of the risks of embodiment: it requires vulnerability and an acceptance of an inherent instability. More often than not, those risks seem almost too much to bear when ministry, on a daily basis, reminds us of our finitude and just how little control we really have. It seems as if embodiment exacerbates what ministry already is—why rub salt into the wound? This is, in part, the truth that *Embody* hopes to tell—that the very people who are called to tend embodiment might be the very ones who reject it. Why? Because ministry is already difficult enough. Why make it more so?

Embodiment means that we could be seen and known. It asks us to be in process and simply to be. Embodiment resists certainty and answers; it values identity, community, and relationship. Once embodiment becomes the primary criterion for leading with integrity, we realize that all ministry is embodied; we realize that the sensual, sensorial, and experiential are just as valuable, perhaps even more so, than strategic plans and vision statements. We are called to ask: What is Jesus disclosing about himself in the body of the text, in the bodies of the text, in your body, in the bodies of your community, and in the body that is the community? We hold that Jesus was fully human and fully divine, but we have a hard time recognizing the implications of this belief. What happens when we separate Jesus's divinity from his humanity? Tending to embodiment—Jesus's and our own—should have implications for how we think about God, pastoral leadership, human dignity, community, justice, and reconciliation. Without embodiment, our ecclesiology, our ministry, and even our theology run the risk of getting over-symbolized or over-metaphorized. The starting point for our leadership matters because it then shapes what will materialize. If we start with revelation, incarnation, and experience, then we are indeed affirming that the "Truth" of God is experiential, not propositional.

The Bible gives witness to embodied experiences of God. In fact, the entirety of the Bible holds this to be true—the writings that make up the library we call the Bible are provisional, incomplete, contingent, immediate, reactionary, occasional, situational; they are not doctrinal or abstract. After all, none of the writers of scripture set out to write with the hope that it would become scripture. We have deemed these compositions scripture by canonizing them. In the end, they are concretizations of experienced faith. Furthermore, the fact that each of these writings is included in the Bible testifies to the universality of its witness. The canonization of scripture held certain standards for inclusion, with one criterion being a writing's appeal to other communities. While we are not privy to the reasons the church at Philippi found it edifying to read Paul's first letter to the Corinthians, we can surmise that there was a sense of shared experience and that there was a perceived connection between the Corinthian experience of God in Jesus Christ and the Philippian witness. In sum, each writing or group of writings in the scriptures should be seen as the articulated faith of the author or of the community who produced it. They are crystalized forms of theologizing, arising from and addressing living communities of faith, thereby bearing witness to profound religious experience.

To lead in the church is to take seriously experiences of God that then can interact with the biblical witnesses and can imagine even contributing to the canon. Rather than theology being something that the church possesses, theology becomes a way of being church and of doing church, whereby the church's actions are indistinguishable from its theological commitments. The church's leadership is undifferentiated from who it believes God to be. We are called to question any and all leadership solutions that are not tested against the gospel's truth. We should ask why there is not a more rigorous critique of the leadership models churches adopt. Are we desperate for anything that might work? Are we so afraid of our future that we are willing to espouse anything that comes along that might promise our future's security?

If we eschew embodiment, then we omit the one leadership characteristic that sets apart leaders in the church from all other kinds of leadership: we are the keepers of the incarnation.

Below is a final blessing for, and on, your leadership:

Blessed Are You Who Bear the Light

Blessed are you

who bear the light

in unbearable times,

who testify

to its endurance

amid the unendurable,

who bear witness

to its persistence

when everything seems

in shadow

and grief.

Blessed are you

in whom

the light lives,

in whom

the brightness blazes—

your heart

a chapel,

an altar where

in the deepest night

can be seen

the fire that

shines forth in you

in unaccountable faith,

in stubborn hope,

in love that illumines

every broken thing

it finds.[3]

—Jan Richardson

---

3. "Blessed Are You Who Bear the Light" © Jan Richardson from *Circle of Grace: A Book of Blessings for the Seasons.* Orlando, FL: Wanton Gospeller Press. Used by permission. janrichardson.com.

Made in the USA
Las Vegas, NV
27 August 2021